IMAGES OF THE NATIONAL ARCHIVES

ARMISTICE

This book is dedicated to the men and women who endured the war. It is for those who gave their lives for it, and for those who had to live with what they experienced. It is for everyone who lost someone in the war.

Their name liveth for evermore.

IMAGES OF THE
NATIONAL ARCHIVES

ARMISTICE

LOUISE BELL

PEN & SWORD
HISTORY

AN IMPRINT OF PEN & SWORD BOOKS LTD.
YORKSHIRE – PHILADELPHIA

First published in Great Britain in 2018 by
Pen & Sword History
An imprint of
Pen & Sword Books Ltd
Yorkshire - Philadelphia

ISBN 978 1 52672 941 5

The National Archives is the official archives and publisher for the UK Government, and for England and Wales. We work to bring together and secure the future of the public record, both digital and physical, for future generations.

The National Archives is open to all, offering a range of activities and spaces to enjoy, as well as our reading rooms for research. Many of our most popular records are also available online.

Typeset in Minion Pro 11/14.5 by
Aura Technology and Software Services, India

Printed and bound in the UK
by CPI Group (UK) Ltd., Croydon, CR0 4YY

Pen & Sword Books Ltd incorporates the Imprints of Pen & Sword Books Archaeology, Atlas, Aviation, Battleground, Discovery, Family History, History, Maritime, Military, Naval, Politics, Railways, Select, Transport, True Crime, Fiction, Frontline Books, Leo Cooper, Praetorian Press, Seaforth Publishing, Wharncliffe and White Owl.

For a complete list of Pen & Sword titles please contact

PEN & SWORD BOOK
47 Church Street, Barnsley, South Yo
E-mail: enquiries@pen-an
Website: www.pen-and-

or

PEN AND SWORD
1950 Lawrence Rd, Havertow
E-mail: Uspen-and-sword@case

CONTENTS

INTRODUCTION

At 11am on 11 November 1918, the fighting on the Western Front ceased. It is on this day and this time that Remembrance celebrations take place every year, as we remember the cost of the First World War, and subsequent conflicts. The events leading up to this, both in 1918 and everything back to 1914, had made a great impact. Towns and cities, especially in France and Belgium, were destroyed; many men had lost their lives; and many more returned from the front lines injured or disabled. The effects and aftermath of this war would be experienced for a long time. Even now, 100 years later, the First World War still holds relevance. A two minutes silence is held every 11 November to mark the Armistice; the Cenotaph and the grave of the Unknown Warrior are prominent symbols in British remembrance. International relationships were shaped and changed by this

Buckingham Palace, Peace Celebrations 1919. *WORK 36/82*

conflict, just as the boundaries and territories of countries did, and the cartography of Europe was remapped.

With the Russians having left the war, the Germans were able to free up more men for use elsewhere. The Treaty of Brest-Litovsk was signed on 3 March 1918, between the new Bolshevik government of Russia and the powers of Germany, Austria-Hungary, Bulgaria, and the Ottoman Empire. The Treaty was agreed upon in order to stop German and Austro-Hungarian forces from making further advances into Russia. The Treaty was a harsh one, depriving Russia of 18 provinces and nearly 30 per cent of its pre-war population.[1] It would later be used against the Germans, when they complained that the Treaty of Versailles was too harsh on them.

The 1918 Spring Offensive, or *Kaiserschlacht*, was a series of German attacks along the Western Front, beginning on 21 March and ending on 18 July. Essentially, Ludendorff wanted to try and break the line held by the British, before the full force of the American troops being sent over could join them. Tactically, the Germans gained a lot of ground in the first of the Offensives and captured numerous prisoners. Throughout this time, the German and Allied forces lost almost equal numbers of men, whether through injury or death. The early success of the offensive gave way to the biggest weakness – the Germans were too exhausted to sustain this level of attack, and their transport was not good enough

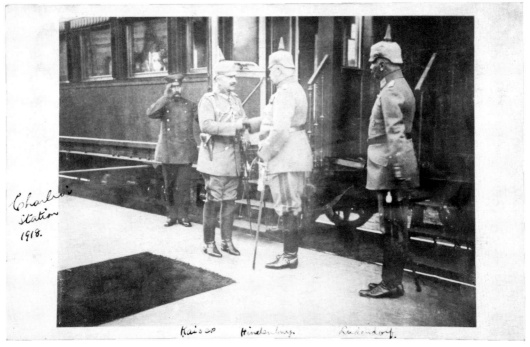

The Kaiser, Hindenburg and Ludendorff returning from the Western Front at Charleroi station, 1918. *RAIL 1020/14*

to get the necessary supplies. They struggled to move both men and guns across the Western Front. The British were badly hurt in this period, but not broken, as the Germans would have wished. Co-ordination in command and operations greatly improved after this, and then came the arrival of the Americans, adding to the number of Allied troops.

1918 saw what came to be known as the Hundred Days Offensive. This was a series of battles which took place on the Western Front between August and November of that year. Following the Allied attacks at the Second Battle of the Marne, from 15 July until 6 August, the British, American, French and Belgian armies mounted a series of their own offensive operations. These would ultimately drive back the Germans from the great gains that they had made during the Spring Offensive, and eventually force the German government to see and agree to peace. On 8 August, General Rawlinson's Fourth Army launched a major attack at Amiens. The Fourth Army had almost doubled in size for the lead up to this, with help from Canadian, Australian and American corps. The battle that followed highlighted how the Allied forces had learned how to successfully combine infantry, artillery, aircraft and tanks into a co-ordinated attack. Attacks made on the Hindenburg Line in September proved successful, and on the 26th, they broke through it. From this point onwards, fighting was still vicious, but the Germans were being pushed further back, until they were forced to accept the terms of peace and the Armistice.

Early on the morning of 8 November, the German Armistice Commission arrived in the small station in the forest of Compiegne. These men had been hurriedly put together, after the Germans had received a letter from Woodrow Wilson stating that he was willing to make peace. Among its 34 clauses, the Armistice contained some major points relating to termination of hostilities on the Western Front within 6 hours of the agreement being signed: the evacuation of occupied France, Belgium, and Alsace-Lorraine within 15 days; and the surrender of machine guns, aircraft, rolling stock, and military stores.[2] Allied troops would also occupy Mainz, Koblenz and Cologne. The naval blockade of Germany was to continue, and hostilities at sea were also to stop immediately. German forces were to evacuate Africa, and the Brest-Litovsk Treaty was to be renounced. There was also to be the immediate release of all Allied prisoners of war, and interned civilians. The German delegation were not happy with all of these terms and were given 72 hours to make a decision on whether to sign. Foch was adamant that there would be no peace unless all of the 34 terms were agreed to. After more early morning discussions on 11 November, finally, at 5:12am, the delegates reached an agreement and the ceasefire document was signed.[3] As we know, the Armistice came into effect at 11am the same morning.

This book will highlight key documents from the collections at The National Archives relating to the Armistice and the aftermath of the First World War. Many of these images will have been rarely seen and will provide key glimpses into what was happening in 1918 and beyond.

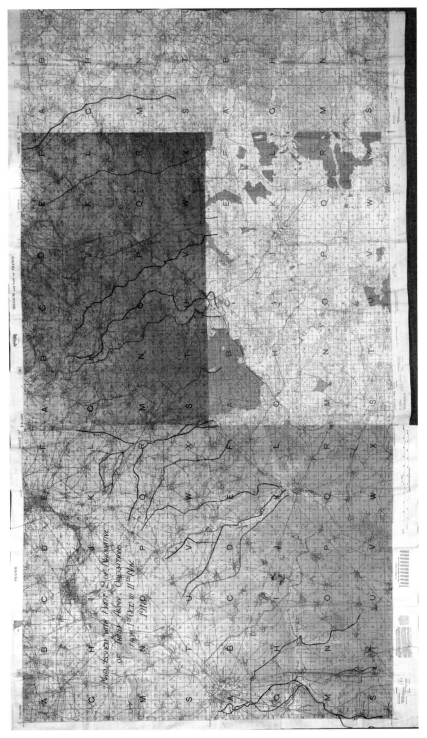

Third Army operations, France-Belgium, October-November 1918. *WO 95/375*

WC 500 B
11 Nov 18
305

(1) The Prime Minister announced that he had received a message from France stating that the armistice had been signed at
5 a.m. that morning, November 11th., 1918, and that hostilities
were to cease six hours later, viz., 11 a.m. He wished to con-
sult his colleagues as to whether the public announcement of the
signing of the armistice should be made at once and the form it
should take.

After a brief discussion the War Cabinet decided —

(a) That the announcement should be made at once
through the Press Bureau, to the effect that
the armistice was signed at 5 a.m. and hostilities were to cease at 11 a.m. today:

(b) That the Commander-in-Chief of the Home Forces
should at once inform all Home Commands, and
should take the necessary steps to celebrate
the news by the firing of maroons, playing of
bands, blowing of bugles, and ringing of
Church bells throughout the Kingdom:

(c) Similarly the First Lord should arrange for
vessels of the Fleet to dress ship:

(d) That the order prohibiting the striking of
Church and other public clocks should be at
once rescinded, the Home Secretary to take
the necessary action:

(e) That the terms of the armistice should not be
made public until they had been communicated
by the Prime Minister to the House of Commons
simultaneously with a similar pronouncement by
M. Clemenceau in the Chamber of Deputies:

(f) The Press Bureau to be informed accordingly.

(2) The First Lord read out a telegram (Appendix I) which had
emanated from the German Warship STRASBURG summoning the German
Fleet to repair to certain stations and be prepared to defend
the Fatherland against the British. The message also called for
a general concentration of German submarines at a northern port.

The Deputy Chief of the Naval Staff pointed out that the
STRASBURG was the ship which had remained loyal longest.

(3) The First Lord read a message he had received from the
First Sea Lord in France (Appendix II), saying that nothing was
known beyond what had appeared in the Press of the present condition of the German Fleet; that the German Army was showing

-2-

Minutes of War Cabinet meeting noting the signing of the Armistice.
CAB 23/14

Buckingham Palace, Peace Celebrations 1919. *WORK 36/80*

CHAPTER 1

TREATIES

'Alas, it is the most serious game ever undertaken, for on the result of it hangs, in my estimation, the future peace of the world.'[1]

This was the response Woodrow Wilson gave to his wife, when she commented that the men trying to sort out terms at the Paris Peace Conference were like little boys playing with toy soldiers. The 'peacemakers' had a great task ahead of them. They not only had to deal with the issues that had caused the war, but also further complications that had arisen from it. So close to Armistice being called, this is a time where countries and people were still very raw about what had occurred. Areas of France and Belgium had been destroyed by the fighting; millions of men had died; and millions more had been wounded and would possibly never work again. The war had cost a fortune in money, also. The British Treasury estimated that victory had cost £24 billion pounds, and the effects on trading patterns around the globe were extensive and long-lasting – and the same applied to economic power.[2]

The Paris Peace Conference ran from 18 January 1919 until 21 January 1920. Initially, the main men involved were the Council of Ten. This comprised the heads of government and foreign ministers of America, Britain, France and Italy, as well as two representatives from Japan. In March 1920, this group divided. The Council of Four were David Lloyd George of Britain, Georges Clemenceau of France, Vittorio Orlando of Italy, and Woodrow Wilson of the United States. These men were the main decision-making body involved up until the Treaty of Versailles was signed. A Council of Five then took on the work after this, dealing with trying to map the new boundaries of Europe and with the next treaty – that with Austria. This five were comprised of the foreign ministers from the above countries: Arthur Balfour (Britain), Stephen Pichon (France), Sidney Sonnino (Italy), Robert Lansing (America), and Baron Makino Nobuaki (Japan).On 28 June 1919, Germany signed the Treaty of Versailles. The rest of 1919 saw two more treaties being signed: that of Saint Germain with Austria, on 10 September; and with Bulgaria on 27 November, referred to as the Neuilly Treaty. 1920 saw two more treaties being signed. The first was at Trianon, with Hungary, on 4 June 1920. And the other at Sevres, on 10 August, with Turkey and Anatolia.

— 1 —

THE UNITED STATES OF AMERICA, THE BRITISH EMPIRE, FRANCE, ITALY and JAPAN,

These Powers being described in the present Treaty as the Principal Allied and Associated Powers,

BELGIUM, BOLIVIA, BRAZIL, CHINA, CUBA, ECUADOR, GREECE, GUATEMALA, HAITI, THE HEDJAZ, HONDURAS, LIBERIA, NICARAGUA, PANAMA, PERU, POLAND, PORTUGAL, ROUMANIA THE SERB-CROAT-SLOVENE STATE, SIAM, CZECHO-SLOVAKIA and URUGUAY,

These Powers constituting with the Principal Powers mentioned above the Allied and Associated Powers,

of the one part;

And GERMANY,

of the other part;

Bearing in mind that on the request of the Imperial German Government an Armistice was granted on November 11, 1918, to Germany by the Principal Allied and Associated Powers in order that a Treaty of Peace might be concluded with her, and

The Allied and Associated Powers being equally desirous that the war in which they were successively involved directly or indirectly and which originated in the declaration of war by Austria-Hungary on July 28, 1914, against Serbia, the declaration of war by Germany against Russia

Tr.

— 3 —

Treaty of Versailles. *FO 93/36/76*

The Treaty of Versailles was signed on 28 June 1919 – a significant date as it marked five years since Archduke Franz Ferdinand had been assassinated at Sarajevo. It was signed between the United States of America, the British Empire, France, Italy and Japan (the Principal Allied and Associated Powers) alongside Belgium, Bolivia, Brazil, China, Cuba, Ecuador, Greece, Guatemala, Haiti, the Hedjaz, Honduras, Liberia, Nicaragua, Panama, Peru, Poland, Portugal, Romania, the Serb-Croat-Slovene State, Siam, Czechoslovakia and Uruguay (these Powers constituting with the Principal Powers mentioned above the Allied and Associated Powers) with Germany.

The main terms were as follows:

The German army was limited to 100,000 men and conscription was banned; all soldiers had to be volunteers.

They were not allowed armoured vehicles, aircraft or submarines.

It was also decided that the Navy could only build six battleships.

The Rhineland became a demilitarised zone, meaning that no German troops were allowed in that area. The purpose of this was to try and make sure that Germany would never pose a military threat to the rest of Europe again. It was also hoped that this forced disarmament would result in other nations doing so voluntarily.

In terms of German colonies and territories:

Alsace-Lorraine went to France

Eupen, Moresnet and Malmedy went to Belgium

North Schleswig went to Denmark

West Prussia and Posen went to Poland

Danzig became a free city controlled by the League of Nations

Memel went to Lithuania

Saar was controlled by the League of Nations (with a vote by the population to be held on the matter after 15 years)

German colonies became mandates under the control of the League of Nations (in practice this usually meant Britain and France)

Estonia, Latvia and Lithuania became independent states (Germany had taken these states from Russia in 1918)

The most famous of the clauses from the Treaty became known as the 'War Guilt Clause'. Essentially, this stated that Germany had to accept the guilt for causing the war. Consequently, this made Germany responsible for paying reparations to the Allied countries, in payment for the huge loss and damage sustained by the conflict. At the time of the signing, it was impossible to state the exact sum that would be required to be paid. However, a year later it was decided that an amount of $33 billion would be set.[3] Economists warned that this would cause huge disruption, but the Allied Powers argued that Germany had to pay, and the Treaty allowed them to take punitive action if the Germans did not do so.

The Treaty of Saint Germain was signed on 10 September 1919 between the United States of America, the British Empire, France, Italy and Japan (again, the Principal Allied and Associated Powers) alongside Belgium, China, Cuba, Greece, Nicaragua, Panama, Poland, Portugal, Romania, the Serb-Croat-Slovene State, Siam and Czechoslovakia (these Powers constituting with the Principal Powers mentioned previously as the Allied and Associated Powers) with Austria.

Some of the main points of the Treaty included a ban on introducing compulsory military service, as well as setting an upper limit of 30,000 men to be allowed in the Army. The Austro-Hungarian Navy was also broken up. As part of this, arms factories were also banned.

In terms of land:

Czechoslovakia, Poland, Hungary and the Serb-Croat-Slovene State were all recognised as independent.

The Austro-Hungarian Empire was dismantled.

Eastern Galicia, Trento, south Tirol and Istria were ceded.

Southern Carinthia went to Austria.

Sopron went to Hungary.

The Anschluss between Germany and Austria was also banned, even though it was argued by the Austrian Foreign Minister, Otto Bauer, that Austria would not be able to survive on its own, and that to avoid economic and social problems, integration into Germany was the only solution.[4]

It was also agreed that Austria would be liable to pay reparations. However, no money was actually received from them.

Map of boundaries of Germany, from the Treaty of Versailles. *FO 925/30129*

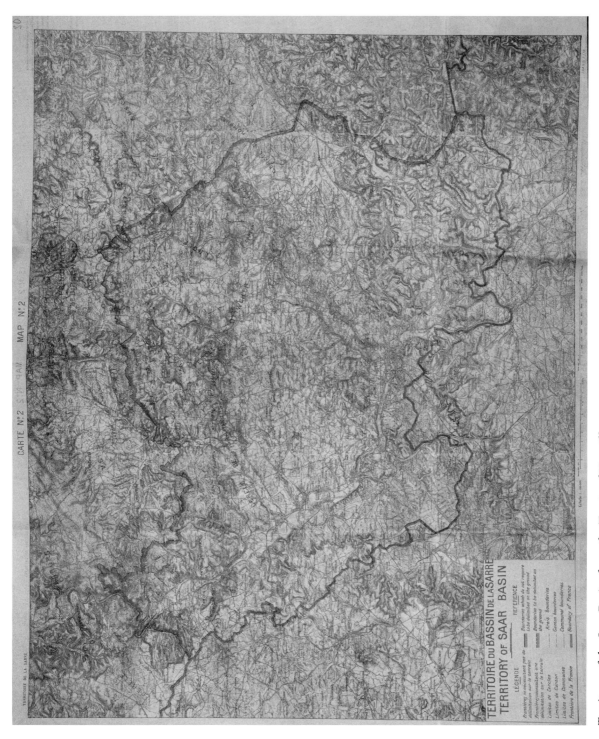

Territory of the Saar Basin, from the Treaty of Versailles. *FO 925/30130*

101

ARTICLE 229.

Persons guilty of criminal acts against the nationals of one of the Allied and Associated Powers will be brought before the military tribunals of that Power.

Persons guilty of criminal acts against the nationals of more than one of the Allied and Associated Powers will be brought before military tribunals composed of members of the military tribunals of the Powers concerned.

In every case the accused will be entitled to name his own counsel.

ARTICLE 230.

The German Government undertakes to furnish all documents and information of every kind, the production of which may be considered necessary to ensure the full knowledge of the incriminating acts, the discovery of offenders and the just appreciation of responsibility.

PART VIII.

REPARATION.

––––

SECTION I.

GENERAL PROVISIONS.

––––

ARTICLE 231.

The Allied and Associated Governments affirm and Germany accepts the responsibility of Germany and her allies for causing all the loss and damage to which the Allied and Associated Governments and their nationals have been subjected as a consequence of the war imposed upon them by the aggression of Germany and her allies.

ARTICLE 232.

The Allied and Associated Governments recognize that the resources of Germany are not adequate, after taking into account permanent diminutions

Treaty of Versailles. *FO 211/517*

102

of such resources which will result from other provisions of the present Treaty, to make complete reparation for all such loss and damage.

The Allied and Associated Governments, however, require, and Germany undertakes, that she will make compensation for all damage done to the civilian population of the Allied and Associated Powers and to their property during the period of the belligerency of each as an Allied or Associated Power against Germany by such aggression by land, by sea and from the air, and in general all damage as defined in Annex I hereto.

In accordance with Germany's pledges, already given, as to complete restoration for Belgium, Germany undertakes, in addition to the compensation for damage elsewhere in this Part provided for, as a consequence of the violation of the Treaty of 1839, to make reimbursement of all sums which Belgium has borrowed from the Allied and Associated Governments up to November 11, 1918, together with interest at the rate of five per cent. (5 %) per annum on such sums. This amount shall be determined by the Reparation Commission, and the German Government undertakes thereupon forthwith to make a special issue of bearer bonds to an equivalent amount payable in marks gold, on May 1, 1926, or, at the option of the German Government, on May 1 in any year up to 1926. Subject to the foregoing, the form of such bonds shall be determined by the Reparation Commission. Such bonds shall be handed over to the Reparation Commission, which has authority to take and acknowledge receipt thereof on behalf of Belgium.

ARTICLE 233.

The amount of the above damage for which compensation is to be made by Germany shall be determined by an Inter-Allied Commission, to be called the *Reparation Commission* and constituted in the form and with the powers set forth hereunder and in Annexes II to VII inclusive hereto.

This Commission shall consider the claims and give to the German Government a just opportunity to be heard.

The findings of the Commission as to the amount of damage defined as above shall be concluded and notified to the German Government on or before May 1, 1921, as representing the extent of that Government's obligations.

The Commission shall concurrently draw up a schedule of payments prescribing the time and manner for securing and discharging the entire obligation within a period of thirty years from May 1, 1921. If, however, within the period mentioned, Germany fails to discharge her obligations, any balance remaining unpaid may, within the discretion of the Commission, be postponed for settlement in subsequent years, or may be handled otherwise in such manner as the Allied and Associated Governments, acting in accordance with the procedure laid donwn in this Part of the present Treaty, shall determine.

ARTICLE 234.

The Reparation Commission shall after May 1, 1921, from time to time,

Treaty of Versailles. *FO 211/517*

LES ÉTATS-UNIS D'AMÉ-RIQUE, L'EMPIRE BRITAN-NIQUE, LA FRANCE, L'ITA-LIE et LE JAPON,

THE UNITED STATES OF AMERICA, THE BRITISH EMPIRE, FRANCE, ITALY and JAPAN,

GLI STATI UNITI D'AME-RICA, L'IMPERO BRITAN-NICO, LA FRANCIA, L'ITA-LIA e IL GIAPPONE,

Puissances désignées dans le présent Traité comme les Principales Puissances alliées et associées;

These Powers being describ-ed in the present Treaty as the Principal Allied and Asso-ciated Powers;

Potenze designate nel pre-sente trattato come le « prin-cipali Potenze alleate e asso-ciate »;

LA BELGIQUE, LA CHINE, CUBA, LA GRÈCE, LE NI-CARAGUA, LE PANAMA, LA POLOGNE, LE PORTUGAL, LA ROUMANIE, L'ÉTAT SERBE - CROATE - SLO-VÈNE, LE SIAM et LA TCHÉCO-SLOVAQUIE,

BELGIUM, CHINA, CUBA, GREECE, NICARAGUA, PANAMA, POLAND, POR-TUGAL, ROUMANIA, THE SERB-CROAT-SLOVENE STATE, SIAM and CZECHO-SLOVAKIA,

IL BELGIO, LA CINA, CUBA, LA GRECIA, IL NI-CARAGUA, IL PANAMA, LA POLONIA, IL PORTOGAL-LO, LA ROMANIA, LO STA-TO SERBO-CROATO-SLO-VENO, IL SIAM e LA CZECO-SLOVACCHIA,

Constituant, avec les Prin-cipales Puissances ci-dessus, les Puissances alliées et asso-ciées,

These Powers constituting, with the Principal Powers mentioned above, the Allied and Associated Powers,

Costituenti, con le princi-pali Potenze suddette, le « Po-tenze alleate e associate »,

d'une part;

of the one part;

da una parte;

Et L'AUTRICHE,

And AUSTRIA,

E L'AUSTRIA,

d'autre part;

of the other part;

dall' altra;

T9.

...

Treaty of Saint Germain. *FO 93/11/74*

The Treaty of Neuilly was signed on 27 November 1919. It was signed between the usual Principal and Allied Powers, alongside Belgium, China, Cuba, Greece, the Hedjaz, Poland, Portugal, Romania, the Serb-Croat-Slovene State, Siam and Czechoslovakia (as the other Powers constituting the Allied and Associated Powers) with Bulgaria.

Under the terms, Bulgaria had to reduce its army to 20,000 men, the border guard to 3,000 men, and the gendarmerie to 10,000 men. The conscript Army was to be replaced by a regular, paid Army. They were denied the rights to possess heavy artillery. Their air force and warships were either destroyed or handed over to the Allied Powers.

In terms of land:

Thrace was given to Greece.

Southern Dobruja was given to Romania.

The Serb-Croat-Slovene State was allowed to expand its eastern borders and therefore received some territory from Macedonia.

All of this meant that Bulgaria lost access to the Aegan Sea.

In terms of reparations, they had to pay 2.25 billion golden francs, as well as giving its neighbours massive benefits such as coal and cattle.[5] A reparations committee was set up in the capital to make sure that they were adhering to these payments.

The Treaty of Trianon was signed on 4 June 1920 between the usual Allied and Associated Powers, with Hungary.

It restricted Hungary's Army to 35,000 men, who could only be lightly armed. It was to be their duty to maintain internal order and secure the borders of the country.[6]

In terms of territories and land:

Czechoslovakia was given Slovakia, the lower part of Carpathian Ruthenia, Bratislava and other small sites.

Western Hungary went to Austria.

The Serb-Croat-Slovene State received Croatia-Slavonia and part of the Banat.

The rest of the Banat went to Romania, as well as Transylvania.
Italy received Fiume.

All in all, Hungary lost around two thirds of its former territory, and an equally large proportion of its inhabitants. With the loss of these territories, Hungary was forced to

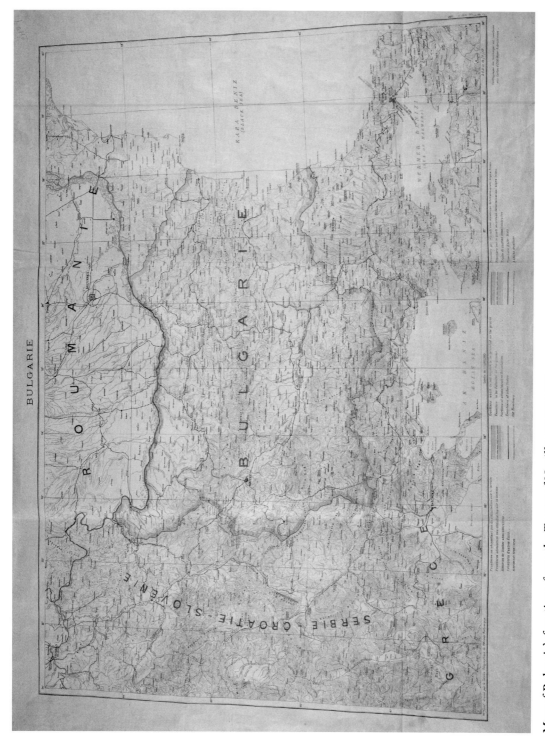

Map of Bulgaria's frontiers, from the Treaty of Neuilly. *FO 925/21109*

reorganise its economy, including increasing foreign trade. Losing much of its mountainous territory meant that it lost a great deal of lumber, coal and other raw materials.

And, finally, the **Treaty of Sevres** was signed on 10 August 1920. This was signed between the Principal Allied Powers of the British Empire, France, Italy and Japan, alongside the usual Associated Powers, with Turkey.

The Treaty essentially abolished the Ottoman Empire. In terms of territories and land:

Turkey was to renounce all rights over Arab Asia and North Africa.
An independent Armenia was established.
Greece would have a presence in eastern Thrace.

The Aegean Islands would also come under the control of Greece.
Rhodes was to go to Italy.

In terms of military, they were allowed to have 50,000 soldiers and 13 boats.

However, this Treaty was rejected by the Turkish nationalist regime, and had to be replaced by the Treaty of Lausanne in 1923. Not strictly speaking part of the Paris Peace Conference treaties, this new treaty constituted an agreement between all powers mentioned above. With this, the war guilt provisions in the Treaty of Sevres were abolished, and the restrictions on the size of the military also disappeared. The provisions made for an independent Armenia were also removed in this new Treaty.[7]

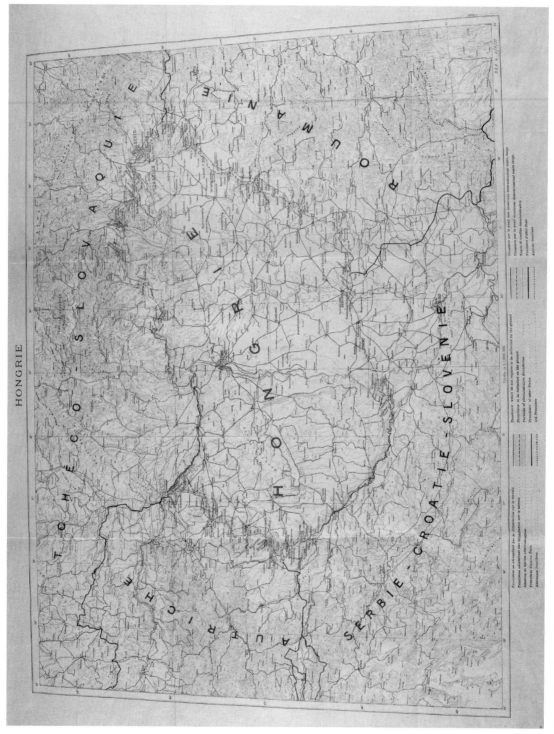

Map of borders of Hungary, from the Treaty of Trianon. *FO 925/20046*

Map showing the demilitarized zones under international control, according to the Treaty of Sevres. *FO 390/2*

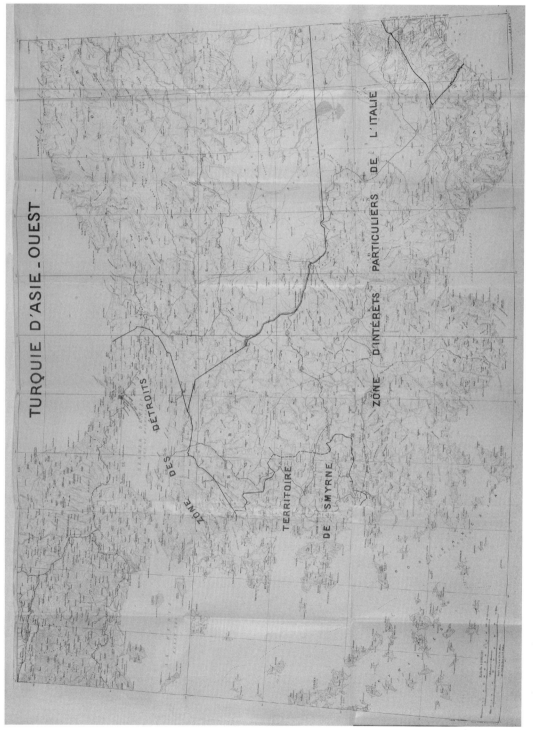

Map showing the partitioning of Anatolia and Thrace, according to the Treaty of Sevres. *FO 390/2*

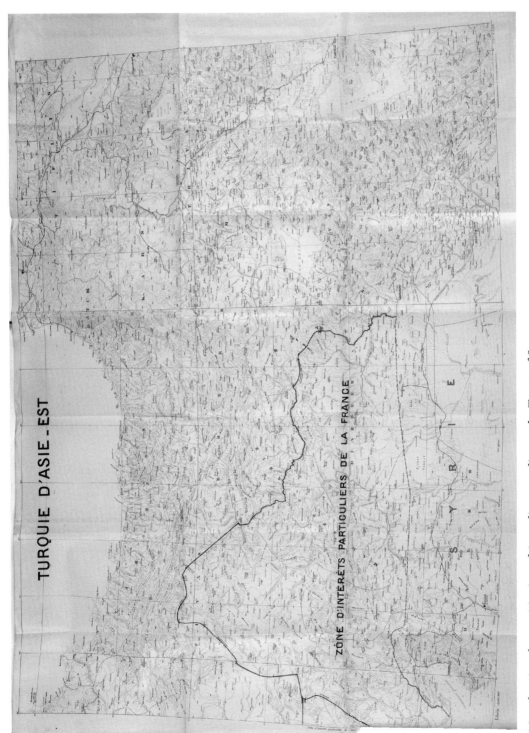

Map showing the partitioning of Anatolia, according to the **Treaty of Sevres.** *FO 390/2*

Map to accompany the Treaty of Lausanne. *FO 925/41330*

CHAPTER 2

DEMOBILISATION

Returning to Britain and civilian life wasn't just something that those disabled by the war had to deal with. Once Armistice was declared, men in the military had to begin the transition back to civilian life also. The process of demobilisation depended on a man's terms of service – in particular whether he was in the regular army, or whether he had volunteered or been conscripted. Naturally, everyone wanted to go home at once but this was not possible, partially due to the time it took to process the men, but mainly due to commitments still ongoing in Russia, Germany and the Empire. Those that were released the earliest tended to be those with much needed industrial skills; and those who had volunteered early in the war. The conscripts were left for last. Even with this, the majority of men were demobbed and back in civilian life by the end of 1919.

SECRET

Appendix to Memorandum (D.M.80) on Transportation and Demobilisation of troops serving in Eastern and Middle Eastern Theatres of War.

Theatre.		No. of troops serving there	Strength of Army of Occupation.	No. of men to be demobilised	Route.	Remarks.
Mesopotamia	British	92,000	40,000	52,000 *	Bombay & all sea route.	* evacuated by 30th April, home by 30th June.
	Indian	260,000	60,000	200,000 *	Direct	* 80,000 evacuated by 30th April, remainder during May and June.
India.	British	95,000	? 75,000	20,000 * plus possible 15,000	all-sea route	* 16,000 Regulars, remainder mainly Territorials or ex-Mesopotamian elements. * evacuated by 30th April; 15,000 expected to start latter part of May.
Egypt (Palestine Syria).	British	140,000	50,000	90,000	Via Taranto or Marseilles	Daily rate of evacuation - 1300 men. 22,317 evacuated by 1st Feb.
	Austr. & N.Z.	22,000	-	22,000	Direct	Monthly rate of evacuation- 3,000 men.
	Indian	100,000	40,000	60,000	Direct	23,300 evacuated by 1st Feb.
Salonika. (Turkey Dobrudja Caucasus)	British	140,000	? 20,000	120,000	Via Taranto	Daily rate of evacuation - 800 men. 30,000 already evacuated.
	Indian	20,000	20,000	-	-	
France & England.	Austr. & N.Z.	195,000	-	195,000	all sea-route via England.	53,000 evacuated by 1st Feb. completion of move not expected before December.
	Indian	12,000	-	12,000	via Taranto	Evacuation to commence when Egypt is nearly clear of Indians already there.
	Chinese	92,000	-	92,000	-	No special arrangements yet made beyond evacuation of those who are approaching the termination of their contract.

Demobilisation of troop from Eastern and Middle Eastern theatres of war. *RECO 1/858*

As this table illustrates, the huge logistical challenge of demobilising the armies of the British Empire was well under way by early 1919. It covers all of the troops stationed in Mesopotamia, India, Egypt and Salonika, as well as the ANZAC, Indian and Chinese troops serving on the Western Front. Although armies of occupation were left behind in many of the former areas of military conflict, the vast majority of troops were speedily released from military service.

However, demobilisation did not occur without some unrest. Disturbances at various army camps occurred at the beginning of 1919, with men complaining about the slow and unfair procedures for demobilisation. This included a mutiny by soldiers at the camp in Calais. Some within government started to fear that the returning soldiers could be rallying points of protest and labour unrest, and fears of Bolshevism amongst them arose. This crisis coincided with major strikes around the country, in particular amongst engineers at Clydeside who were demanding shorter working hours. During 1919, nearly 35 million days were lost to strikes. In 1920, this amounted to around 29 million.[1]

Despite this, there were plans in place to help the demobilised men return to the labour market and gain employment. The Ministry of Labour helped devise schemes for the ex-serviceman to get back into work. A training scheme from 1919 begins with stating some of the issues surrounding these men returning back to Britain:

> 'You cannot put the clock back four years, take men from the Army or the Navy or the Air Force and simply put them where they were before the War, for the reason that you cannot put back a man's age.'[2]

The problem was deemed to be particularly difficult for the young, educated men who had been on the threshold of a career when they abandoned their studies and went to war. One who went straight from school at age 18 into the military could not easily return to school and pick up where he left off and complete his studies in the normal way. Yet, if he were to offer himself for professional employment, he would be rejected on the basis that he was unqualified. The employer could not entirely be blamed in this situation, as it was natural for him to want a skilled worker for skilled work, and he could not very well take on someone deemed unskilled. Of course, after the war, finding someone who was qualified for some jobs became increasingly more difficult. For over four years the supply of male workers had been diminished, but now that there was a ready supply of men again, many of them were unskilled. During the war period, many women took up work in factories and in the various trades that men left behind – as well as taking up uniformed roles such as the Women's Royal Naval Service and the Queen Mary's Army Auxiliary Corps. Women also worked extensively in the medical services, both at home and at the Front. By the middle of the war, around 75,000 were in the employment of the munitions industry.[3]

Womens' Land Army girls with piglets. *MAF 59/3*

Following is an example of commonplace work that women had to take over whilst the men were occupied elsewhere. By 1916, steel companies were beginning to complain about the shortage of supplies of limestone being supplied to them by Buxton Lime Firms. The firm said that this shortage was due to the lack of workmen left at the company – by February 1916, over 600 of their men had joined the Army.

Accordingly, like many firms in Britain during this period, Buxton Lime Firms employed women. There does not seem to be very much information about this undertaking, except for a few notes scribbled on the back of the wonderful collection of photographs that we have of women working there. From these, we know that women worked in the following areas:

- tree felling and wood cutting for quarry and colliery timber
- dry walling
- joinery
- agricultural work

- the rabbit section (associated with the British Rabbit Society)
- the goat section (affiliated with the British Goat Society and National Goat Society)
- painting trucks

Many issues surrounded the men coming back from the various theatres of war. Some men had not begun training before the war; the training of others had been interrupted; some were forced to seek new jobs due to disability; and even those who had had sufficient training before the war found themselves to be out of touch with their work and that their knowledge was rusty. But just how could these educated men be re-absorbed into the labour market? The solution was the Training Scheme devised by the government. The object of this scheme was to:

'assist those educated ex-servicemen, whether commissioned or otherwise, who for one good reason or another are unfitted immediately to occupy salaried positions, to train for suitable careers. And where necessary grants are made to approved candidates for the payment of their fees and for their own maintenance, during the period of training.'

[*Photo Topical Press*

Driving a Motor Van

Woman driving a motor van, 1917. *MH 47/142*

'Learn to make munitions' poster. *EXT 1/315*

Women workers at Buxton Lime Firms. *MUN 4/671*

Chemical laboratory. *LAB 2/1516/DRA128/30/1918*

Through this scheme, it was hoped to assist those who were, on every ground, entitled to assistance, and to recreate this cohort of trained men who were suited to more skilled jobs in business, professional and technical areas.

The report states that this was 'essential to the country's well-being'.[4] This scheme was to be administered by three different departments:

1) The Appointments Department of the Ministry of Labour acted as a general clearing house for all candidates and dealt with all cases of training in offices, works, and with private employers generally. In addition, it would administer the training in all cases where the man was disabled.
2) The Board of Agriculture, with its Scottish and Irish offices, dealt with all cases of agricultural training.
3) The Board of Education, which also had Scottish and Irish offices, administered training in universities, colleges and schools, and anything that generally fell under the category of higher education.[5]

The work undertaken by the Appointments Department would rely heavily on employers co-operating and offering training vacancies. It would also have responsibility for determining how suitable a candidate was for training in the career that he desired to follow. Interviewing Boards were set up to help with this process and had some 1,200 leading business and professional men on hand to help staff these and give their opinion on suitability.[6] In order to safeguard the interests of the candidates, every potential opportunity was examined and verified before it was added to the list of official vacancies. Therefore, both candidate and training opportunity were approved before either could be taken further forward. The scope of the training courses was wide. For example, under the heading of Architecture there was: general, ecclesiastical, marine, draughtsmanship, building and building research, concrete work, carpentry and joinery, town planning, and land and mine surveying. With such a wide range in just one speciality, it can be no surprise that training could be offered in everything from banking and engineering, to advertising and optics, and geology and veterinary science.

A limited number of British ex-officers and other ranks could, if they had served in the Navy, military or air force during the war, receive assistance from Imperial funds to allow them to pursue courses at universities and other approved institutions within the overseas areas of the British Empire. The grant given to these men would be enough to provide for maintenance during the course, including holidays, and for his tuition fees, after taking into account their means from other sources. There were six universities that could be attended in Australia – Sydney, Melbourne, Adelaide, Tasmania (Hobart), Queensland (Brisbane) and Western Australia (Perth). Between them, the usual sorts of degrees could be studied, ranging from the Arts, law and medicine, to engineering and dentistry. In some places, special concessions were made for those who were ex-servicemen, i.e. only having to pay half fees.

Moving to Canada, there were a much greater number of universities that could be attended. The universities there excelled particularly in engineering and agriculture. Therefore, the student could really pick a university based on which province he would like to reside in. There were also an abundance of agricultural colleges that could be attended, if the student so desired. The fees there varied, and there appears to have been no special provisions for these men, unlike in Australia. But the fees were still cheaper than in Britain.

The University of New Zealand had four different colleges attached to it: University of Otago; Canterbury College; Auckland University College; and Victoria University College. Degrees and diplomas in the Arts, science, medicine and surgery, and journalism could be studied, to name but a few. Again, fees to attend any of these varied.

The University of South Africa had six colleges attached to it, which were given permission to establish facilities and departments that they saw fit. Still, the usual degrees in Arts, science, medicine, law, engineering, etc. could be found here. There were also agricultural colleges specialising in areas such as wine farming and tobacco.

At the University of Hong Kong there were faculties of Arts, science and medicine. The Universities of India were mainly examining and degree-granting bodies, with each having a large number of affiliated colleges. Finally, the University of Malta had faculties in literature, science (which included engineering and architecture), theology, law, and medicine. With such a large number of agricultural training opportunities available abroad, there was a push to try and make men who desired to undertake this training stay in Great Britain.

Again, financial assistance was offered to undertake the training. This could take two forms: residential training with selected farmers in England and Wales; or agricultural scholarships at approved universities or colleges in England and Wales. The grants for farm training were intended primarily for those ex-servicemen who were selected as suitable but could not undertake training without government assistance. For an unmarried officer, the grant would not exceed £125 per annum, for two years, and £130 per annum for married officers.[7] In the case of married ex-officers, an allowance not exceeding £24 per annum could also be made in respect of each child under 16 years old, up to a maximum of £96.[8]

Spraying fruit trees. *LAB 2/1516/DRA128/30/1918*

This scheme did not apply to Scotland and Ireland, and any officer who desired to undertake agricultural training in these two countries had to go through a different process, and fill out the relevant forms for whichever place.

For Scotland, the Board of Agriculture were offering scholarships to one of three agricultural colleges, varying in value from £25 to £175 per annum, depending on the needs of the applicant.[9] Allowances of between £48 to £125 were also on offer for those wishing to undertake practical training on farms.[10] As with England, an allowance would be made to trainees married before 11 November 1918, of £24 per annum for each child under the age of 16, up to a maximum of £96.[11]

In May 1919, the following statistics were produced, with regards to progress of this scheme (in England and Wales):

Applications refused by Board - without reference to County Committee – as obviously ineligible: 30

Applications referred by Board to 58 County Committees

- demobilised officers: 801

- non demobilised officers: 589

'Officer pupils' started training in 39 Counties: 264"

'Provisionally' approved (in addition) by County Committee: 307

'Officer pupils' left training in 2 Counties: 2

Applications refused by County Committees: 130

Applications withdrawn by applicants: 92

Applications outstanding for interviews etc. by County Committees: 595[12]

On 2 October 1919, the average weekly number of applications for agricultural training was stated to be 130.[13]

A letter from Field Marshal Douglas Haig, who was serving as Commander-in-Chief Home Forces by this time, in November 1919, intended to be published in various newspapers around the country, stated that 90 per cent of those who had been demobilised in the past year had already been reabsorbed into civilian life. This seems like a very positive figure, but the letter continues with the following information: some 20,000 ex-officers and other ranks on the registers of the Appointments Department, and between 300-400,000 other ex-servicemen on the registers of the Employment Department, were still unemployed.[14] The letter further goes on to say:

'I desire on this first anniversary of the Armistice to pay respectful tribute to those public-spirited Employers who have already given substantial evidence of their sympathy for the ex-service Officer and Man, and at the same time to make a personal appeal to each Employer to remember that the unemployment of lack of training of these men is due to their military service: to reflect on what the nation owes to them: and to consider whether he cannot apply to the Appointments Department or to the Employment Exchanges and, by taking into his employment one or more of these 400,000 ex-service Officers and Men, collaborate, even at some immediate personal sacrifice in their resettlement before the winter has set in.'[15]

A lot of press surrounded these training schemes; with a great deal of it being more on the negative side. More than one piece appeared in *The Times* in November 1919, referring to the schemes as 'Official Waste' in the headlines.[16] Criticisms came of the sometimes inability to match a man with a job that would be equal to the rank he held whilst in the Army. Examples cited are officers being recommended as hotel porters and window

Milking a cow. *LAB 2/1516/DRA128/30/1918*

Drawing office. *LAB 2/1516/DRA128/30/1918*

Hand-loom weaving. *LAB 2/1516/DRA128/30/1918*

cleaners, according to the writer. There were also cases where the men seemed not to have received the grants owed to them for their training, and newspaper articles referred to them as 'poverty-stricken'.[17] However, the newspapers also highlight the provisions made to get the message of these schemes out there to the ex-servicemen. Public meetings were held in the North, and talks were given in military hospitals (e.g. Ripon, Catterick, Newcastle, York, Leeds and Sheffield) to those men convalescing there, to let them know what was being done to help them return to civilian life.[18]

CHAPTER 3

WOMEN'S UNIFORMED SERVICES

Women's work in munitions and in the medical services has already been mentioned. However, one area that became more important as the war progressed was that of the auxiliary military services that women were enrolled in. The idea behind these was to replace men in non-combatant roles and therefore free up more men for the Front. Women could enrol in the Women's Army Auxiliary Corps, the Women's Royal Naval Service and the Women's Royal Air Force. This section will focus on these three services – looking at how they were formed and why, taking the story through to their disbandment at the end of the war. It is important to understand the roles these women played during the war, in order to understand the impact of demobilising these services, and to add further poignancy to their inclusion in Armistice celebrations.

> 'The Air Service is urgently in need of women workers – so urgently that every fit woman who is not already doing work of national importance should feel that a direct personal call has come to her.'[1]

On 1 April 1918, alongside the Royal Air Force, the Women's Royal Air Force (WRAF) was formed. Personnel of the Women's Army Auxiliary Corps and Women's Royal Naval Service were given the choice of transferring to the new service and over 9,000 decided to join. Civilian enrolment swelled WRAF numbers. They were dispatched to RAF bases, initially in Britain, and then later to France and Germany in 1919.

As with other services, the period of service was stated as 12 months, or for the duration of the war, whichever one turned out to be greater. Age restrictions were in place for candidates wishing to join. For overseas service, you had to be at least 20, and for home service, 18.[2] Again, as with other female services, there were two categories, mobile and immobile. The former could work anywhere in Britain and were also eligible to be sent overseas; the latter would work locally. No member whose husband was serving overseas would be eligible to serve in the same theatre of war as he did. If the husband was subsequently ordered to the same theatre of war, then the WRAF member would be withdrawn from that area and sent elsewhere.

There were certain occupations where, if the woman was already employed in one of these, she would not be allowed to serve in the WRAF unless she brought a letter from

'Women come and help' poster. *EXT 1/315*

her employer stating that she had permission to do so. Some of the occupations that came under this restriction were: school teaching; work in VAD, military, Red Cross and civilian hospitals; munitions work; and government service. There were also restrictions relating to the nationality of the woman (or of her parents or husband). Candidates, unsurprisingly, had to be medically fit and undertake medical examinations. And finally, one of my favourite parts of enrolment into women's services, they had to provide two references, one of which had to come from another woman.

The Conditions of Service for the Immobile Branch (those who would stay at home and work in an area they lived in or near – essentially, local service) states that 'women are urgently needed to release fit men for active service', which was a common line used in the recruitment for all the women's services in the First World War. These women were required for various branches of technical work on aeroplanes, and as motor drivers and cyclists. Apparently, no woman should feel that this service was not for her due to lack of skills in these areas – training would be provided. During this period, they would be paid learners' rates. Women were also required as cooks and waitresses, and for household duties in the messes.

The areas of work that could be undertaken were split into four categories:

- clerical
- household
- general
- technical

The clerical section included clerks, shorthand writers and typists. Cooks, waitresses, laundresses and domestic workers came under the household section. The general section included storehouse women, tailors, shoemakers, telephonists and motor cyclists. And finally, the technical section encompassed jobs such as motor car drivers, photographers, fitters, metal workers, aeroplane riggers, wireless mechanics, and many more.

At the end of the war, a lot of debate seemed to surround what should happen to the WRAF and whether or not it was worth keeping some women in employment at air bases. In 1919, there was a lot of argument within the air ministry about the future of the WRAF. In October 1919, Hugh Trenchard, later described as the 'Father of the Royal Air Force' argued the following:

'It is absolutely necessary to retain a certain number of W.R.A.F.s for Cooks in hospitals. The Doctors are insistent that they must be under some sort of discipline, and though we are trying to train Cooks it is not easy to do in so short a period. Therefore I wish for sanction to keep up to 300 W.R.A.F.s as cooks or clerks until at least April 1st, 1920.'[3]

However earlier in the year, arguments such as the following were made for keeping women around:

'My reasons for advocating a permanent W.R.A.F., are:-

1. They are generally speaking, highly efficient, if perhaps, a little more expensive than man power.
2. In the event of mobilization, the employment of women on a large scale will be required, and we shall have a nucleus of a highly efficient and well trained organization on which to expand.
3. At large establishments I think that they tend to improve the general welfare of the men, in the matter of dancing and concerts etc., more especially in the big establishments which are situated at some distance from a town.'[4]

Despite these arguments, the WRAF were disbanded in 1920, although with the outbreak of the Second World War, the Women's Auxiliary Air Force (WAAF) was founded.

Women working on airship construction. *AIR 1/2307/215/19*

The Women's Royal Naval Service (WRNS) was founded in November 1917. The intention was for them to undertake shore-based duties, in order to free up sailors to go to sea. 'Free a man for sea service' was a slogan commonly found on recruitment posters. The terms and conditions booklet for the WRNS starts off with the following sentiment:

'The Women's Royal Naval Service has been formed because there are certain duties, hitherto performed by men of various naval ranks and ratings, which can be done equally well by women, whose substitution will release men for more strenuous branches of naval service.'[5]

The first director of the WRNS was Dame Katherine Furse. Furse was initially a member of the Voluntary Aid Detachment (VAD) and on the outbreak of the war she was chosen

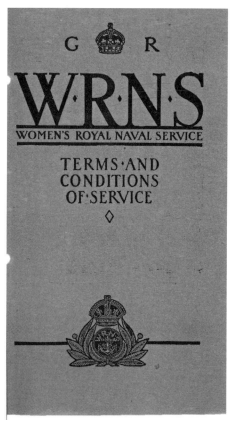

Above left: Women's Auxiliary Air Force recruitment poster, WW2. *INF 3/118*

Above right: Term and conditions of serving with the Women's Royal Naval Service. *ADM 116/3739*

to head the first VAD unit sent to France. Aware of her administrative abilities, the authorities later placed her in charge of the VAD department in London. However, she was unhappy about her lack of power to introduce reforms. In November 1917, she and several of her senior colleagues resigned, due to a dispute over the living conditions of the VAD volunteers and the Red Cross's refusal to co-ordinate with the Women's Army group. Almost immediately after this, she was offered the post of director of the WRNS.

Both officers and ratings were classed as either 'mobile' or 'immobile'. Immobile ratings were most often found in London, or at naval bases such as Portsmouth.

Initially, WRNS undertook domestic duties such as cooking and cleaning. But this later expanded to a greater variety of roles, such as that of wireless telegraphist or electrician. Most were given a trade category, and these were denoted by blue, non-substantive trade badges which were worn on the right arm. The main trade categories were as follows:

scallop shell = household worker

three-spoked wheel = motor driver

arrow crossed by lightning flash = signals

crossed keys = storekeeper; porter; messenger

envelope = postwoman; telegraphist

crossed hammers = technical worker

star = miscellaneous

In terms of the actual enrolment into the WRNS, the forms seem particularly lengthy. Of course, one had to answer the usual questions of name, date of birth, age, address. Nothing out of the ordinary for today. There are also many statements that one had to agree to, such as:

'Do you agree that in the event of your being guilty of any act or neglect in breach of this contract or of any of the rules, regulations or instructions laid down from time to time for this Service, you will be liable to a fine?'[6]

There are quite a few statements relating to the potential of being fined.

The initial application form also has a host of questions relating to areas such as the nationality of your mother and father at birth, nationality of your husband, and so on.

One area which really highlights the perceived differences between men and women in these services lies within the medical forms that women had to complete. The forms start

MII.   W.S. 45

WOMEN'S ROYAL NAVAL SERVICE.

MEDICAL SCHEDULE OF EXAMINATION ON ENTRY.

of Board... Medical Registration No..................

ame...

.ge .... { Parish ....

ate and year of Birth .... } Birthplace { County ....

.ddress ....

....

Married................................ Single..............................

Widow .... Children ....

lature of Proposed Occupation ....

'revious Occupation ....

lave you previously been medically examined for entrance }
to a public Service, or by a Medical Board ? ....}..............

QUESTIONS AS TO GENERAL HEALTH.

lave you ever had :—

(1) Any serious illness or accident ?...

(2) Any serious operation ?...

(3) Rheumatic Fever or Pleurisy ?..

(4) A Fit or Faint ?..

(5) Have you ever been absent from your work for more }
than a month at a time, on account of illness ?.......}................

(6) Have you ever spat blood ?..

(7) Are your periods regular ?...

Date of last period ?...

Does your period interfere with your work ?................................

Candidate's Signature..................................

Date ....

CONCLUSION.

General Impression ....

Medical History..

[1175] 7982/31137 10m 5/18s 71153 G & S 110

Examiner's Initials ....

Medical form for joining the Women's Royal Naval Service. *ADM 116/3739*

off as one would expect, with questions relating to any recent serious illness or accident. But as the questionnaire continues, questions start to take on a different tone than what would be required of their male counterparts. This begins with questions regarding fits and fainting. However, the most personal come in the form of those relating to menstruation:

'Are your periods regular?

'Date of last period?

'Does your period interfere with your work?'

Just imagine if that was asked nowadays.

When the First World War came to an end, the WRNS were disbanded. By the end of this period, they could count some 5,500 members. They were reformed for the outbreak

Members of the Women's Royal Naval Service marching in the Victory Parade, 1919. *WORK 21/74*

Women's Royal Naval Service, WW2. *INF 3/686*

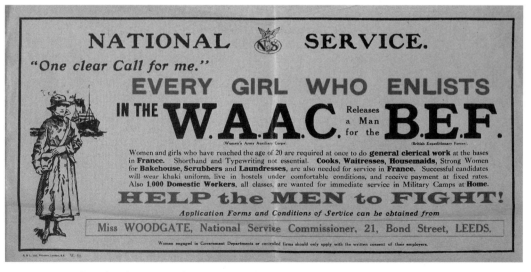

Recruitment flyer for the Women's Army Auxiliary Corps. *NATS 1/109*

Women's Royal Naval Service, WW2. *INF 3/112*

of the Second World War. This time they had an even more varied list of activities which they could undertake. These new roles included responsibilities such as radio operators, meteorologists and bomb range markers. At their peak, in 1944, the numbers of WRNS officers and ratings were 74,000. After the Second World War, a small number of permanent WRNS positions were retained (3,000 of them). These were mainly administrative and support roles at Royal Navy establishments, both in the UK and overseas.

The service was finally integrated into the Royal Navy in 1993, when women of any rank were able to serve on board naval vessels as full members of the crew.

The Women's Army Auxiliary Corps (WAAC) was formed following Lieutenant General Lawson's report of 16 January 1917, which recommended employing women in the army in France. February 1917 saw the appointment of Mona Chalmers Watson as the Chief Controller, and the appointment of Helen Gwynne-Vaughan as the Chief Controller

Overseas. Recruiting for the WAAC officially began in March, with the first draft enrolled on the 28th of that month. The first draft then embarked to France three days later. Even with this first draft in place, the Army Council Instruction (no. 1069) which formally established the WAAC was not issued until 7 July.

Although it was a uniformed service, there were no official military ranks within the WAAC. The equivalent of officer was officials, and these included: chief controller, deputy chief controller, assistant controller, unit administrator and deputy administrator, and so on. The other ranks were referred to as members. Members were made up of subordinate officials, forewomen, and workers. Workers were the lowest grade. Promotion within the ranks was rare, and if occurred was more likely to be from worker to forewoman, than for a member's rank to an official's one.

Enrolment came through similar forms as the other women's services. The form included questions about her age, her marital status, her nationality, and the nationality of her parents. They also had to confirm that they would be liable to scrutiny under a small section of the

Women's Auxiliary Corps leaving Cardiff by train, 1917. *NATS 1/1307*

Army Act. As with the sister organisations, work was essentially mobile or immobile. Much of the emphasis was on women going to France, but there were also members required for home in Britain.

In terms of the work that was undertaken, like their sister services in the WRAF and WRNS, the WAAC were not there to fight. They were organised into seven sections:

- clerical
- household
- mechanical
- telephone and postal
- miscellaneous
- general
- technical

Jobs ranged from motor drivers and cooks, to telephonists and telegraphists.

In appreciation of its good services, it was announced in April 1918 that the WAAC were to be renamed the Queen Mary's Army Auxiliary Corps (QMAAC). Approximately 57,000 women served with the WAAC and the QMAAC during this conflict. However, like everyone else, demobilisation began with the declaration of Armistice. On 30 April 1920, the QMAAC were disbanded. A small group had remained in St Pol to help with the work of the Graves Registration Commission, but this unit too was disbanded at the end of September 1921.

CHAPTER 4

DISABILITY

'There was not so much red-tape to go through in August, 1914, when the country was crying for men and I left a good job to join the soldiers, but now when I am a maimed and not fit for manual labour, this country has no further use for us. Yet it was to be a country fit for heroes to live in.'[1]

These are the words of disgruntled ex-serviceman Thomas Kelly, a private in the Gordon Highlanders and a man who returned from the First World War in receipt of a 100 per cent disability pension after having both of his legs amputated above the knee. Kelly's situation was not a unique one, but one that was shared by nearly 6 million British and German men, disabled by injury or disease in this period.[2]

Training schemes to aid men such as Kelly were set up throughout the country. Many were linked to the more prominent limb-fitting hospitals, such as Erskine and Roehampton. Initially, Kelly received 12 months of training in boot repairing under the instruction of Bailie McIntosh, Bootmaker, a private employer, in Stirling. However, even with such training, he was never able to obtain employment as a boot repairer and was advised that he was unfit for such work. In a letter, he states that 'The late Sir Wm. Macewen told me to give up as he said I was not fit for it.'[3] Kelly received no pay during this training period except a one-off sum, essentially to keep him motivated. He was, however, receiving a full disability allowance at this time. The main issue surrounding this time was that Kelly's legs had had to be amputated to within 5 inches of the hip joint, leaving him practically helpless. As a result, he could not be sent to a regular training centre and so he was eventually able to persuade McIntosh to take him on, as the repair shop was so close to where Kelly lived:

'Mr McIntosh says he was at very considerable expense teaching him having to lift him off his chair and on again, hand him tools etc., and could not afford to pay him anything like 15/- [shillings] per week although he gave him something.'[4]

COPY.

5 Glen End,
Old Kilpatrick,
Dumbartonshire.

22.9.25.

Sir,

    With reference to letter I got regarding training at
Erskine, I would like to know what right you have to
know about the business I had in Stirling. It was my own
money that I earned and saved up when I looked after the
canteen in Erskine House. It cost me close on £100
to stock my shop, when I started and it was two years
after when I got £40 from the Harry Lauder Fund. I put
it in stock which is not much in tobacconist and newsagent
line As regards the boot repairing, I think you got a clear
enough answer at your meeting at Glasgow. There was not
so much red-tape to go through in August, 1914, when
the country was crying for men and I left a good job to
join the soldiers, but now when I am a maimed and not fit
for manual labour, this country has no further use for
us. Yet it was to be a country fit for heroes to live in.
I think you will better let me know if you are going to
give me training - yes or no. Then I will know how to
act by writing to His Majesty and explaining my case to
him and I might get some satisfaction.

I remain,

(Sgd.) THOMAS KELLY.

Letter about training for a disabled ex-serviceman. *LAB 2/1195/TDS2884/1919*

The Stirlingshire Local Committee referred to this as a very exceptional case and wished for it to be treated as such:

'The special idea of the Committee was to give Kelly such a training that he could employ his time usefully and have a healthy interest in life. Mr McIntosh certified that he can do repair work and it has been reported to the Committee that he intends to undertake this work on his own account.'[5]

McIntosh was apparently aggrieved that he had not been paid for the training that he had delivered. It was further stated that 'in Kelly's state he could not work such regular hours as a man in good health and certainly his training gave a great deal of work to Mr McIntosh.'[6] McIntosh himself states that in the last few months of training, Kelly started to improve and made 'good progress' and learned to use the tools well.

Not one to give up, it appears, Kelly then turned his attention to opening his own business, in the form of a Tobacconist and Newsagent's, in 1921. Funded with his own money, he later received a grant for £40 to assist with keeping the business going. The grant came from the Harry Lauder Million Pound Fund For Maimed Men, Scottish Soldiers And Sailors, set up by the well renowned Scottish singer and comedian, who had a great deal of sympathy, and evidently support, for those who had been significantly injured in the war. Unfortunately for Kelly, he had to give up this business – he gave it to his sister, as it was not proving to be very profitable. Yet, once more, he shows a desire to be able to undertake some form of employment, which brings us to back to his letter regarding his desire to carry out more training – this time in the form of basket making, at Erskine House. It is not just this one letter that Kelly sent with regards to this. The file contains numerous letters from him, badgering about whether or not he will be allowed to undertake such training – once again showing his determination.

That he wanted to do this training at Erskine is significant; this facility was one of the leading in Great Britain with regards to limb production and rehabilitation. Workshops were erected in the grounds of hospitals in order to try to aid men with finding employment, and decent employment at that, once they had left the wards. Not just intended as a forward-looking scheme, the workshops were detailed with the task of employing the spare time of those waiting for treatment at the hospital in 'useful and remunerative work'.[7]

No mention is made of whether or not Kelly received artificial legs. With such a small stump left, it would suggest that the answer to the question of whether he did or not would be no – this is furthered by the fact that McIntosh had to help him move around, and that he seems to have become very immobile, in general. The war definitely made the need for a strong prosthetic limbs industry very apparent. Around 41,000 servicemen returned

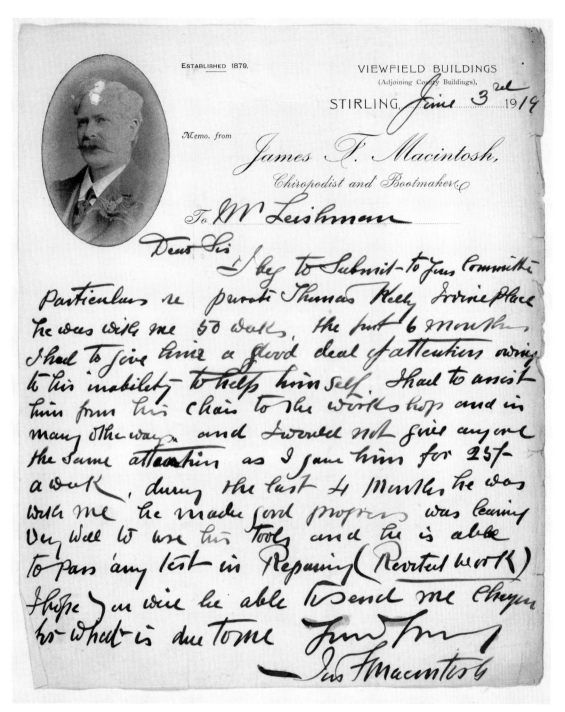

ESTABLISHED 1879.

VIEWFIELD BUILDINGS
(Adjoining County Buildings),

STIRLING, June 3rd 1919

Memo. from

James F. Macintosh,

Chiropodist and Bootmaker.

To Mr Leishman

Dear Sir

I beg to Submit to your Committee particulars re private Thomas Kelly Irvine Place he was with me 50 weeks, the past 6 months I had to give him a good deal of attention owing to his inability to help himself, I had to assist him from his Chair to the work shop and in many other ways and I would not give any one the Same attention as I gave him for 25/- a week, during the last 4 Months he was with me he made good progress was learning Very Well to use his tools and he is able to pass any test in Repairing (Riveted work) I hope you will be able to send me Cheque for what is due to me Yours truly

Jas F Macintosh

Letter from employer of a disabled ex-serviceman. *LAB 2/1195/TDS2884/1919*

Form TR. 3.

Application for Sanction to the Training of a Discharged Disabled Sailor or Soldier.

This Form is for use in those cases only where the training
is **not** being given under a course or scheme of training for
which the Local Committee has already received sanction
either from the Statutory Committee or the Ministry of
Pensions.

It is essential that all the information requested be
given on this form in order that delay may be avoided.

The Local Committee for *Stirlingshire (Central)* hereby apply for the
sanction of the Minister of Pensions to train a disabled man, particulars of whose
case are given below :—

1. Name and Address   *Kelly – Thomas*   No. *6776*
   27 Irvine Place, Stirling

2. Regiment or ship   *Gordons*

3. Age   *25*

4. Whether married or single   *Single*

5. Date of Discharge   *31/7/17*

6. Whether in receipt of :—
   (a) Disablement pension   *27/6 for life = 100 %*
       (Rate of pension should be stated)
   (b) Gratuity awarded under Art. 7 (1) of the Royal Warrant
       (Amount of gratuity should be stated)

7. Occupation and wages prior to enlistment   *Miner – £2·10/- p w k*

8. Present occupation, if any, and wages   *None*

9. Disability   *Loss of both legs*

10. Whether disability is such as to prevent   *Yes*
    his resuming his former occupation

Particulars of the proposed course of training.

1. Institution, factory or workshop at which training is to be given   *Private workshop – James F Macintosh Boot & Shoemaker Stirling*

2. Branch of trade to be taught   *Boot & Shoemaking*

Duration of proposed course   *12 mts*

proposed to be paid   *None*

Application form for the sanctioning of training for a disabled ex-serviceman. *LAB 2/1195/TDS2884/1919*

from the war missing one, or more, limbs.[8] This equated to around 11,600 arm cases and 29,400 leg cases.[9] When the war broke out, the making of prosthetic limbs was a very small industry in Britain. In 1916, Britain was wholly dependent on foreign limb makers.

With hospitals opening solely with the task of helping these limbless men, it was important that workshops for the production of artificial limbs were set up in Britain, in increasing numbers than there had been previously. British limb makers were employed as much as possible with the hope of continuing this practice, by training some of those who received such limbs, so that they could aid in the making of limbs for those who would follow. However, it did become essential to bring in those from abroad (such as Carne from the USA).

The 'Humana' foot was created by a company originating in St Louis, Missouri. It is particularly interesting to see the different materials being utilised in the manufacturing of such a foot (fibre, aluminium, wood and felt) – as opposed to just wood, as limbs were initially made from. Experimentation with newer, and potentially lighter, materials became more common towards the end of the war and after. The company themselves state that they have developed this new type as 'extreme lightness' was the main objective.[10] The same file also contains images of men wearing artificial legs – one can see where the limb is held on with the use of a shoulder strap, in the images where the men are without trousers.

These also highlight how it would have been possible to hide such a limb, when fully clothed. Yet, if a limb was not properly fitted, then all of this would have been for naught. In order for these men to be able to have a chance at returning to some approximation of their pre-war lives, it was important that they were able to use the limb effectively and comfortably. Therefore, the fitting of a limb was a lengthy procedure, one that involved waiting for the stump to heal properly and have enough time to shrink to the size that it would remain, and then the leather bucket of the leg (or arm) could be fitted effectively for that man. Experiments with materials such as certalmid (a mixture of glue, muslin and celluloid) and light metals were starting to be undertaken as the war came to a close. Yet these mostly had to wait until the 1920s, to be experimented with fully. Correspondence exists from 1920 which indicates that, in the December, plans were underway regarding the building of new sheds, on site at Roehampton, for the production of certalmid sockets for limbs.[11] Yet, much of this is more concerned with the costs of preparing these sheds than with the actual production of the sockets. In June 1918, the *Evening News* reported on a new artificial arm, created by A.C. Adams, which was made of aluminium and steel, and weighed only 2lb. 3oz.[12] Despite its lightness, the arm was still strong enough for men to undertake any number of tasks. A description of it also stated that, 'The arm is so jointed that when the man walks it swings naturally and is scarcely distinguishable from a sound limb.'[13] Aesthetics were not the be all and end all of having a new limb fitted, but the more life-like quality that this limb possessed would surely have made it a popular one. The use of a light metal limb versus that of a wooden

A happy "family party"

Baskets grow under his quick fingers

A shop to be proud of

Cycling baskets are in great demand

A quiet game with 'raised' dominoes

When he has shown you the shop in which he makes his baskets and trays, this St. Dunstan's craftsman will next take you into the beautifully situated home overlooking the sea, which St. Dunstan's found for him, and display the cups which he won for rowing. This man has even more than the usual reasons for being grateful to St. Dunstan's, for his eyesight went gradually after the War, and if he had not discovered that the famous organisation looked after cases like his as well as after the men who were blinded outright, he would not have known where to turn. As a St. Dunstaner, however, he now rests content in the knowledge that he will be looked after and cared for as devotedly in the future as in the past and the present.

Rehabilitation at St. Dunstan's. *PIN 15/1061*

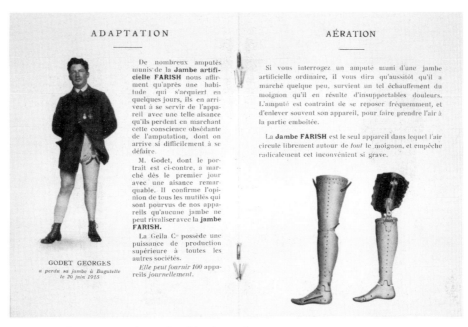

Pamphlet from a French artificial limb production company. *MUN 7/285*

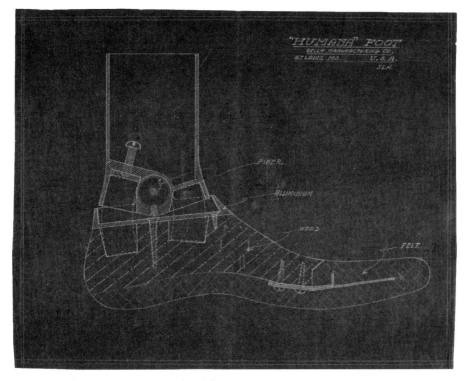

Blueprints for the Humana artificial foot. *MUN 7/285*

Men wearing artificial limbs. *MUN 7/285*

limb was something to which great consideration was given. A light metal limb was believed to require fewer repairs than that constructed from wood; as well as the positive that a metal limb tended to weigh less than a wooden one. Mr. Corner, a well-known London surgeon, and former consulting surgeon to the hospital at Roehampton, stated that over 90 per cent of men who had suffered from above-knee amputations had greatly benefitted from the use of a light metal limb.[14] He believed that the metal limbs were easier to learn to use, and that those who did use them were found to be more physically fit than those who wore wooden legs.[15] Still, even then, there were still men to be found who preferred the wooden leg over the newer metal ones.

Standardisation of limbs came gradually. It was not until the beginning of the 1920s that the government research laboratory finished designing what would become known as the 'Standard Wooden Leg'; something which was to be manufactured by all limb makers, from a prescribed pattern.[16] The question of standardisation was something that received the close attention of experts from the middle of the war onwards, but as 1918 was drawing to a close, there had still been no agreement on a design that would be suitable to meet the criteria of being named the 'standard limb'.[17] A committee, which had been set up by the Ministry of Pensions, did consider the standardisation of components of limbs, to aid with making repairs easier. Artificial limbs were more often than not repaired by someone other than the original maker, and such differences could affect the

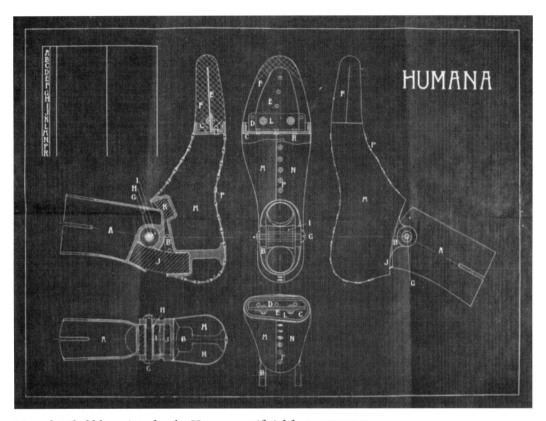

More detailed blueprints for the Humana artificial foot. *MUN 7/285*

quality, and the length of time it took to repair a limb. It was argued that there was no sense in standardising a pattern for the construction of limbs, when there were constant improvements being made in designing prostheses. An article in the *Morning Post,* dated December 1918, retorted that to delay the standardisation 'until perfection has been reached means that those of us who may have lost our limbs will be much too dead to enjoy the perfected standardised limb which some day will be produced'.[18] With so many limb makers working in Britain at this time, it would be difficult to gain consensus as to which was the best limb to use as the so-called 'standard' type. Each maker would naturally believe that his was the best, and that he could make the furthest advances in the designing of limbs. The quantity of makers also meant that repairs, renewals, and adjustments all took time, as they tended not to be too fond of, or all that great at, working on goods that someone else had manufactured.[19] This was deemed unfair for the men who had to wear these prostheses, as it resulted in discomfort for them and caused a general sense of dissatisfaction. Eventually, William Macewen, the eminent surgeon, and

Blueprints for standardised parts of artificial limbs. *MUN 7/285*

one of the founders of the hospital at Erskine, with his set of artificial limbs that could meet practically every need, managed to persuade the government to adopt a number of standardised designs, despite the 'opposition of the Whitehall bureaucracy'.[20]

However, once standardisation came into play, there were still causes for dismay. Standardisation brought with it images of mass production and of everything being the same, and perhaps not being of the greatest quality.[21] This went against the idea of limbs being fitted and constructed especially for the soldier. Many believed that this would result in all amputees receiving the same limb, no matter of their height, their weight, or what area of the limb that the stump began.[22] However, this was not what was meant, at all. Parts of the limbs would be constructed to the same specifications, and using a certain range of materials and parts, but they would still be 'made to measure'.[23] No two stumps were the same; therefore, no two artificial limbs could be identical. The principles that Erskine and Roehampton had announced they would adhere to upon their openings, regarding the proper fitting of limbs, were something that were still very much in place. In order to aid men in this new employment, equipment and tools were adapted, which can be seen most prominently in those who had lost an arm. In 1918, the Science Museum in London undertook some observations regarding how the body is utilised when using certain tools. Photographs were taken of a man as he used the most common tools that might be required for any of the trades being taught. These photographs were then examined to understand the different angles and movements that the body makes when working, and these were, in turn, used to inform the adaptation of tools for the men who had lost limbs.

The same file also contains blueprints and sketches of how these tools could be adapted. On the sketch overleaf, you can clearly see where the apparatus would be attached to a stump of the upper arm.

Shrapnel from exploding shells, and bullets from machine gun fire, destroyed the flesh of these men fighting and left behind some of the worst injuries ever seen. 'The only thing I dread is losing a limb – I'd far rather be killed!' was a common cry amongst those fighting on the front lines.[24] The fear of the helplessness that would come with losing a limb appears to be greater than that of losing one's life. This 'utter lack of precious independence which the loss of a limb suggests' was something that could be dealt with, however.[25] The so-called

Investigations into arm and hand movements for artificial limbs whilst using hand tools. *MUN 7/331*

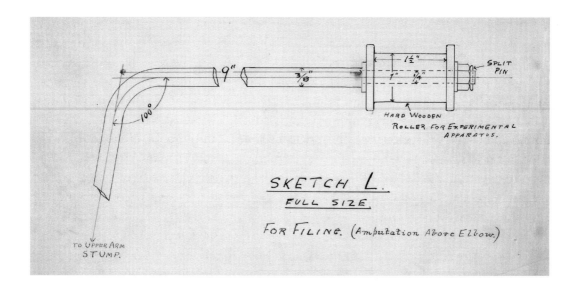

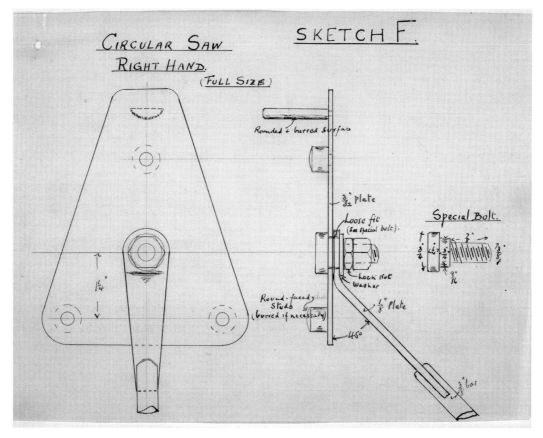

Adaptation of hand tools for use with artificial limbs. *MUN 7/331*

helplessness that these men feared did not have to be permanent, unlike the loss of their lives. The many men who returned from the Front missing a limb was something which both the British government and health professions would have to deal with. Hospitals were set up to try and aid with the increasing number of limbless men who were being sent back to Britain. Numerous convalescent homes were also set up for those who were awaiting the fitting of artificial limbs. These were mainly set up within various stately homes and country mansions, which were taken over for the duration of the conflict, and after. But it was the opening of hospitals specifically to aid and care for those who needed new limbs and needed help with rehabilitation and the use of such limbs, that were of great importance. Various hospitals, such as the Edinburgh War Hospital, in Bangour, and Shepherd's Bush Military Hospital, in London, had wards dedicated to such undertakings. Yet it was the establishment of the Princess Louise Scottish Hospital For Limbless Sailors And Soldiers at Erskine House and the Queen Mary Convalescent Auxiliary Hospital at Roehampton, which had some of the greatest impacts; as well as being two of the most well-known of the hospitals dedicated to such a task.

Rehabilitation fell under two different strands: either that of sport and recreation, or that of work and employment. Both seem to have inherent masculine qualities about them. This idea of usefulness surrounds the theme of rehabilitation, but was this usefulness in regards to the well-being of the man or was it more a means of making sure he was still a contributor to the economy? Jeffrey Reznick argues that providing these men with this sort of work would aid them in becoming 'healthy individuals', 'able-bodied breadwinners' and 'productive citizens'.[26] Writing in 1918, John Galsworthy, known as an author, but also someone who campaigned greatly for the rights of disabled servicemen, argued that:

> 'Of little use of man to nation would be the mere patching up of bodies, so that, like a row of old gossips against a sunlit wall, our disabled might sit and weary out their days.'[27]

Playing sport was one manner in which people with disabilities could subscribe to the 'norms' of society. There was also the added bonus of higher fitness levels achieved through sport, and the social aspect of getting together with other people and enjoying an activity such as football. Julie Anderson argues that the sporting needs of civilians with disabilities were not well catered for, and those activities that were run were organised by voluntary groups.[28] Yet, during the war, and after, sporting events in which the war disabled took part were widespread. These events were organised partly to raise money for the hospitals and institutions that cared for the men, but also as a means of allowing the disabled men to show off their sporting ability to the public. Many of these men had to remain in hospital

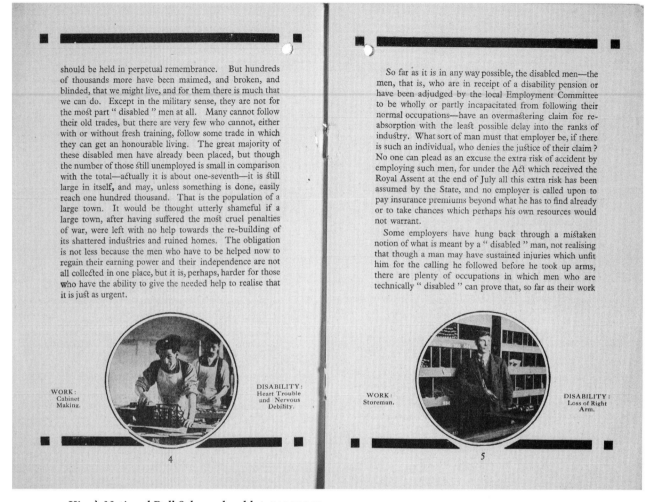

should be held in perpetual remembrance. But hundreds of thousands more have been maimed, and broken, and blinded, that we might live, and for them there is much that we can do. Except in the military sense, they are not for the most part " disabled " men at all. Many cannot follow their old trades, but there are very few who cannot, either with or without fresh training, follow some trade in which they can get an honourable living. The great majority of these disabled men have already been placed, but though the number of those still unemployed is small in comparison with the total—actually it is about one-seventh—it is still large in itself, and may, unless something is done, easily reach one hundred thousand. That is the population of a large town. It would be thought utterly shameful if a large town, after having suffered the most cruel penalties of war, were left with no help towards the re-building of its shattered industries and ruined homes. The obligation is not less because the men who have to be helped now to regain their earning power and their independence are not all collected in one place, but it is, perhaps, harder for those who have the ability to give the needed help to realise that it is just as urgent.

So far as it is in any way possible, the disabled men—the men, that is, who are in receipt of a disability pension or have been adjudged by the local Employment Committee to be wholly or partly incapacitated from following their normal occupations—have an overmastering claim for re-absorption with the least possible delay into the ranks of industry. What sort of man must that employer be, if there is such an individual, who denies the justice of their claim ? No one can plead as an excuse the extra risk of accident by employing such men, for under the Act which received the Royal Assent at the end of July all this extra risk has been assumed by the State, and no employer is called upon to pay insurance premiums beyond what he has to find already or to take chances which perhaps his own resources would not warrant.

Some employers have hung back through a mistaken notion of what is meant by a " disabled " man, not realising that though a man may have sustained injuries which unfit him for the calling he followed before he took up arms, there are plenty of occupations in which men who are technically " disabled " can prove that, so far as their work

WORK: Cabinet Making.

DISABILITY: Heart Trouble and Nervous Debility.

WORK: Storeman.

DISABILITY: Loss of Right Arm.

4

5

King's National Roll Scheme booklet. *LAB 20/366*

for lengthy periods of time, so the chance to play a sport was one manner of breaking up the monotony of ward life. Sport was also a part of service life. It maintained fitness levels, enforced discipline, and allowed for the idea of being part of a team to grow. The ability to take part in sports, even after injury, allowed these men to return to this feeling of belonging; it enforced the idea of something masculine. It allowed the chance to prove that disability had not 'affected his interest or ability on the quintessentially masculine playing field'.[29] There was also the allowance of the opportunity to return to something that would have likely been part of their pre-war life; a return to normality. These men could play anything from football to cricket to golf. Not just for fun, it also allowed men to practice using their new limbs.

Newspaper cutting about a sports day for limbless ex-servicemen. *PIN 38/474*

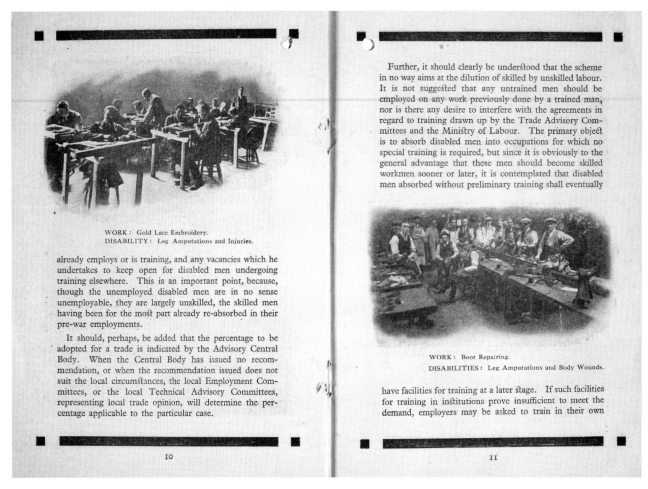

King's National Roll Scheme booklet. *LAB 20/366*

Numerous trades were taught in workshops set up in these institutions. At Erskine, the main departments within the workshops were cabinet making and carving, boot making, tailoring, basket making and hairdressing. However, anything from bookkeeping to bricklaying to driving could be undertaken in the various workshops that sprang up. Similarly, workshops were erected in the grounds of Roehampton. Instruction in various work was available, with accounts talking of motor and electrical engineering, carpentering, accountancy, shorthand and typewriting.[30] Twenty-four trades in total were available to practice in these workshops.[31] Men were able to learn new trades or practice with the hope of returning to the trade in which they were employed before war broke out.

Whether Thomas Kelly secured further employment is not revealed within his file. However, for many men who returned from the Front with a missing limb, the outcome was more positive. At the end of 1923, the Ministry of Labour reported that 28,051 firms were now enrolled in the King's National Roll Scheme. This was started in 1919, as a means of attempting to gain more employment for more disabled ex-servicemen. The scheme essentially asked employers to sign up (it was their choice to do so – this was not a mandatory scheme) and pledge to employ disabled ex-servicemen as 5 per cent of their workforce. Many employers were encouraged by the advertising of the scheme as a means of helping those who had served their country. Also, employers on the roll could display a crest and were given preferential consideration for government contracts.

Similar institutions were set up for men who suffered from other effects of war, such as shell shock and blindness. St Dunstan's was the most famous for men who had lost their sight and ran similar rehabilitation programmes as to those at the hospitals for limbless men.

Set up in 1916, the Ministry of Pensions took over the powers to make pension awards to those who suffered disablement due to, or aggravated by, their military service. Criteria for eligibility were seriously revised. Previously, they had been based on a veteran's ability to earn a living wage; now they were granted on the basis of a standardised schedule. For example, the loss of two or more limbs entitled a man to a full pension; where as something like an amputation below the knee was assessed at 50 per cent. Psychological issues such as neurasthenia and shell shock were much harder to categorise. Debates surrounding what constituted shell shock arose within the medical profession – some wanted to confine it to symptoms that appeared only after a man had been rendered unconscious by shell explosion, but the same symptoms were obvious in men who had only been exposed to shell fire and the traumas of battle, but hadn't been rendered unconscious.[32]

Shell shock is one of those issues that many think of when they hear the First World War. Perhaps one of the most famous cases is that of the well-known poet Siegfried Sassoon.

This letter was sent to the editor of *The Nation,* a leading British radical weekly newspaper, one week after a poem by Sassoon had been published within its pages. The poem in question is entitled 'I Stood With The Dead' and is a definite statement against the war. The last verse describes the poet standing amongst the corpses at the Front, lamenting that these men were being paid to stand in line and to kill and to die. The letter was sent to the editor to ascertain whether or not Sassoon was fit to be back at the Front. If he had written the poem in 1918, when it was published, there were fears that he should not have been sent back to France after his stay at Craiglockhart.

To get to this point in the story, it is worth briefly looking at Sassoon's service in the war. On 4 August 1914, he attested with the Sussex Yeomanry. By May 1915, he had been commissioned into the 3rd Battalion Royal Welch Fusiliers, as second lieutenant. In the November of the same year he was posted to the 1st Battalion and sent to France.

Sample certificate for those taking part in the King's National Roll Scheme. *LAB 20/366*

[*Sport and General.*

Bootmaking at St. Dunstan's.

or downhearted, to grumble or to complain, just quietly to think of our blinded soldiers in Regent's Park, learning to earn their daily bread.

"When the whistle blows in the workshops, you see them lay down their tools, put on their coats, and then—with hands stretched out in front of them, and feet shuffling on the ground—they grope their way out, feeling their way through the darkness, starting when they strike a table, laughing when they collide with one another. It is only then that you realise that they are blind.

"'This place,' said Mr. Pearson, 'is the happiest house in London; probably in the whole world. And I'll tell you why. It's full of sympathy.'"— From *Lloyd's Weekly*, by HAROLD BEGBIE.

9

'Our Blinded Soldiers and Sailors' booklet. *PIN 15/1054*

Telephony for the Blind.

London is wonderful and bewildering, and in the workrooms there is laughter, cheery happy voices, and chaffing and whistling, for happy sound has to be substituted for happy sight, and a more cheerful set of fellows over their work it would be hard to find. In one corner of the long gallery shoes are being re-soled with a solidity and finish that many a full-sighted cobbler might envy. Further along doormats are being made—firm and solid ; no amateur work this, but stuff to compete with any anywhere ; and baskets of every conceivable shape and size, good and well finished and serviceable ; and on the other side of the room a carpenter's bench, where frames are being turned out that would not disgrace the most lynx-eyed workmen. One watches with amazement, not only the precision of direction, the sureness of touch,

5

'Our Blinded Soldiers and Sailors' booklet. *PIN 15/1054*

knew that her father, side by side with David Lloyd George, had taken twenty years ago a far stronger line against the Boer War. But they were not sent to prison by the then Government, which was wise in its generation. Is the present Prime Minister likely to win this war by sending to prison an English girl because she presumes to challenge militarism without asking the leave of his Censor? Is he not rather in danger of destroying that long fought-for right of the English race to write and speak what they choose, or to be charged and tried by a jury of their fellow countrymen if their writing or speaking is alleged to be contrary to law? The only trial these three Friends have had is a trial by one worthy Alderman with an appeal to another worthy Alderman; not very satisfactory, when such a grave issue is at stake, even though the Aldermen had legal advisers.—Yours, &c.,

Ex-M.P.

THE FUNDS OF THE BRITISH WORKERS' LEAGUE.

Sir,—In this week's issue you are good enough to devote some little attention to the British Workers' League, and in the course of the article to which I refer, you ask certain questions and make certain assertions with regard to this organization. Perhaps you will permit me briefly to comment thereon.

You ask, "What is our financial basis?" To that question I beg to state that every farthing of money we have is received absolutely without any conditions whatever, on our published programme, and every receipt issued to subscribers is issued with that proviso.

Our funds are under the control of two trustees, quite unconnected with party politics, men of irreproachable standing, one of whom has served his country gloriously in the war, has been grievously wounded, and has been decorated by the King. This gentleman has long family associations with Liberalism. Our other trustee is an agricultural expert of national repute. These facts were published in our official organ, the "British Citizen" on March 16th.

From the beginning of our propaganda up to the present moment, we have not obtained a farthing from any political party, or other organization. May I, in my turn, inquire respectfully, why you should make these innuendoes alone against the British Workers' League? The writer of the article in question might perhaps, with some use, pursue his inquiries in other directions. For instance, he might get into touch with Mr. George Lansbury and inquire of that eminent rebel and Syndicalist, how he manages to continue the publication of the "Herald" and to support the propaganda of the "Herald" League from the pennies and halfpence of his wild supporters. The "Herald" is reputed to have a very large circulation, but practically has no revenue from advertisements; unlike almost any other paper in the kingdom, it continues to appear week-by-week at the pre-war price of 1d., with paper five times the price before the war, and printing charges increased three or four hundred per cent. How is it done?

Perhaps your tearful contributor will follow up my suggestion and pursue his inquiries in that direction. Our chief sin seems to be that we are prepared to learn the lessons of the war and decline to bend the knee to the blessed gospel of Cobdenism, sans phrase, for which heinous offence we are apparently a "counter-revolutionary body." If to seek to substitute a system of national and imperial economy for the pre-war system of cosmopolitan economy is to be reactionary, then indeed I must plead guilty. If to desire a reconciliation between the administrators of industrial capital and the manual workers on the basis of a guarantee of high wages, is, in the view of the Old Liberals, contrary to the spirit of Liberalism, then indeed we have departed far from the blessed teachings of the leaders of Victorian economics, whose names the writer of the article quotes with such unction.

I make no complaints whatever, that you stand pre-eminently for Individualism, Cobdenism, Free Trade, and Pacifism, as against our faith in the new Empire Democracy, based on national economics; but I hope I am not asking too much of you as an honorable opponent, with lofty ethical ideals of internationalism, to fight "clean," and to refrain from publishing totally baseless innuendoes against men and women, every bit as good democrats as yourself, but who visualize the coming democracy in very different terms from those expressed by the bourgeois Gradgrinds of Victorian capitalism.—Yours, &c.,

Victor Fisher, Hon. Sec.

[Mr. Fisher has not answered the question whether the funds of a body describing itself as a "Workers' League" are in any degree derived from sources which could be described as the bourgeois Gradgrinds of Georgian capitalism.—Ed., The Nation.]

RUSSIAN AND BRITISH DEMOCRACY.

Sir,—May we bring to your notice that a number of Russians living in London have formed a Union, "Russian Commonwealth" ("Narodopravsto"), with the object of uniting Russians who—

1. Repudiate the so-called Bolshevik rule as tending to disintegrate the Russian state and as endangering the independence of the people of Russia.

2. Advocate the summoning of a democratically elected Constituent Assembly as the only expression of the free will of the whole people.

3. Consider the republican order to be the surest guarantee of the peaceful and free development of Russia, and

4. Believe that only in close union with the Allies can Russia regenerate her strength and avert the menace of German domination aggravated by the whole foreign policy and orientation of the present rulers of Russia, of which the Brest Litovsk peace is the most disastrous expression.

One of the chief aims of the Union is to promote the closest possible rapprochement between the British and Russian democracies.—Yours, &c.,

Committee.

Prof. S. P. Turin (Chairman).
J. Y. Shklovsky-Dioneo (Vice-Chairman).
Prof. S. I. Gavriloff.
A. M. Krougliakoff.
D. V. Filitz.
E. I. Zoundelevitch (Hon. Treasurer).
A. R. Bagaturianz (Hon. Secretary).
Sardinia House, Kingsway, W.C. 2.

PROPAGANDA IN PICTURES.

Sir,—It occurred to me that among those whose sentiment your paper represents, some protest might be made against one of the latest small incitements to misery and madness flung to the hopeless public.

The Ladies' Emergency Committee of the Navy League has exhibited, broadcast in some parts of London, a paper appealing for funds to help British prisoners, and showing a German woman in nurse's uniform pouring water upon the ground, before the eyes of helpless wounded men. The grace and gesture of the woman depicted suggest truly enough the mental condition in which such a deed must be done. It is the grace of a moral maniac—a creature in whom the propaganda of hate, together perhaps with personal loss and suffering, has unseated reason and conscience, and let loose forces of inhuman malice such as sleep perhaps in all of us. The purpose of the committee, whose merciful work everyone must value, is no doubt to excite compassion for prisoners suffering among callous foes, but it is grievous that in stimulating compassion their poster should at the same time tend so strongly to arouse in the spectator the same passion of vindictive ferocity whose existence among the enemy has cruelly affected our own men.

There has been kindness as well as inhumanly shown by the enemy to our prisoners, and ferocious treatment of innocent aliens among ourselves has not been unknown; but the unreflectiveness of the average man leads him readily, on representation of some atrocity, to take it as typical of a whole nation, and to make his enemy alone the representative of those evil forces that universally beset the struggling spirit of man. He who gazes absorbed upon evil thus projected is transformed into its likeness, malice and hatred rising unreproved within his own breast. It is for this reason that such pictures, influencing even children whom one would wish to shield from the worst contagion of war, are so greatly to be regretted.—Yours, &c.,

M. Bodkin.

50, Southwood Lane, Highgate.

THE LATE REV. DR. JOHN HUNTER.

Sir,—It is intended to produce a short biography of the late Rev. Dr. John Hunter. I should be grateful if any who possess letters from him or other relevant material would allow me to see them. They would be carefully handled and returned.

I should also be glad if any who knew him in his early days in Aberdeen or at college, or were acquainted with his work in York and Hull would write to me.—Yours, &c.,

L. S. Hunter.

8, Prince Arthur Road, Hampstead, London, N.W. 3.

THE LEWIS SEYMOUR CASE.

Sir,—I beg to acknowledge your memorandum and cheque for £159 5s., which The Nation has collected to defray part of the expenses in the trial, Moore and Heinemann v. Lewis Seymour. On Mr. Moore's behalf and my own, I offer you our grateful thanks.—Yours, &c.,

W. Heinemann.

20-21, Bedford Street, London, W.C. July 3rd, 1918.

Poetry.

I STOOD WITH THE DEAD.

I stood with the Dead, so forsaken and still:
    When dawn was grey I stood with the Dead.
And my slow heart said, "You must kill, you must kill;
Soldier, soldier, morning is red."

On the shapes of the slain in their crumpled disgrace
    I stared for a while through the thin cold rain. . . .
"O, lad that I loved, there is rain on your face,
    And your eyes are blurred and sick like the plain."

I stood with the Dead. . . . . They were dead; they were dead.
    My heart and my head beat a march of dismay;
And gusts of the wind came dulled by the guns.
    "Fall in!" I shouted; "Fall in for your pay!"

Siegfried Sassoon

Siegfried Sassoon poem 'I Stood With the Dead'. *WO 339/51440*

Once there, he became known for reckless acts of bravery, which eventually led to him being awarded the Military Cross in July 1916.

Throughout his military career, Sassoon had a few hospitals stays. But it was the one in July 1917 which became the most significant. The cause for this admission was stated as: mental breakdown. Coinciding with this was Sassoon's statement against the war in which he argued that he could no longer be party to the political mistakes and insincerities for which the men were fighting and suffering. He also wanted to highlight the atrocities to all at home, who could not imagine the horrors of the Front. Instead of court martialling Sassoon for this, he was sent to Craiglockhart War Hospital in Edinburgh to undergo convalescence – because surely such an outcry against the war could only come from someone whose mind had been influenced by the war and therefore he could not be held responsible for what he had said.

Concerned that his words would be seen as those of a mad man, Sassoon decided that he had to go back to the Front, whether he wanted to or not. A medical board in November 1917 declared that he was fit for general duties again, and by May 1918 he was back serving on the Western Front. The fear that the poem published in *The Nation* was written during this time, when the war was still being fought, was that Sassoon's mind might still be in chaos and that he could not be trusted with men's lives or trusted not to spread his anti-war sentiment. In his response, the editor of the newspaper does not reveal how long the poem had been in his possession for, before he printed it.

Two years after the Armistice, around 65, 000 ex-servicemen were drawing pensions for neurasthenia – of whom 9,000 were still undergoing hospital treatment.[33] It was in 1920 that the war office set up a committee to investigate shell shock and how it was dealt with. This came after Lord Southborough initiated a debate in the House of Lords on 28 April of the same year. Following this, the Committee were given the following terms of reference for their work:

'To consider the different types of hysteria and traumatic neurosis, commonly called "shell-shock"; to collate the expert knowledge derived by the service medical authorities and the medical profession from the experience of the war with a view to recording for future use the ascertained facts as to its origin, nature, and remedial treatment, and to advise whether by military training or education, some scientific method of guarding against its occurrence can be devised.'[34]

The War Office Committee of Enquiry into Shell-Shock met officially from 7 September 1920 until 22 June 1922. The founding of this committee made the issue of mental health and war a political one, as well as a personal one. The Committee comprised 15 members, ranging from those who were medically trained to those who represented the military. There were also prominent doctors who dealt with neurology – Sir Frederick W. Mott and Dr W. Turner.

THE YORKSHIRE OBSERVER,
TUESDAY, MAY 28, 1918.

THE TREATMENT OF SHELL-SHOCK.

WORK OF THE BRADFORD HANDICRAFTS CLUB.

If you walk down the south side of Forster Square you will pass under a quaint signboard. Painted, as the mediæval artists have it, "in proper colours," the chains by which it hangs are still bright, and the drab pall of soot and dust has not yet descended upon its bright surface. So it swings bravely over a little door, upon which are painted the words "Khaki Handicrafts Club." Turn in and ascend two flights of stairs, and you will find you have climbed back through as many centuries of social history. The Industrial Revolution has been passed midway on the journey; Arkwright and Stephenson have yet to be born; you are back in the age when craftsmanship was the honoured sister of art. About you, however, are relics, or, rather, wrecks of the very latest phase of civilisation—soldiers in hospital blue. Some are making purses, using a leather thong instead of waxed thread; others are making string bags, either with a netting needle and mesh or by macramé knots; others, again, are making raffia-work baskets, and a few are weaving borders for shopping bags, or embroidering cushion covers with gay-coloured silks.

The reason for their uniform is not immediately apparent. Watch this man by the pillar netting a bag. He passes his needle full of string through the loop in his last row of work, and round the mesh to form a new loop. His thumb then descends upon the mesh to hold the string from slipping while he makes his knot and pulls all tight. No Yarmouth or Galway fisherman could work more neatly. But look closer; look particularly at his hands, and you will see his thumb, broad and strong as it is, tremble ere it closes on the mesh; you will see his needle-point waver uncertainly ere it finds the loop. The mischief is out. These men are suffering from shell-shock, and shell-shock being a diablerie peculiar to twentieth-century warfare, their presence in this secluded corner of medieval industry points an ironic comment on our vaunted progress.

HANDICRAFTS FOR SHELL-SHOCK.

The value of handicrafts in the treatment of shell-shock, albeit generally admitted, is in no danger of being overrated. Work at some craft is made part of the treatment at most military hospitals, but, owing to lack of proper accommodation, proper facilities for instruction, and the absence of all that arouses enthusiasm in the men, it falls oft-times into a position of secondary importance, or is crowded out altogether. A band of public-spirited ladies in Bradford, keen craftswomen, realised how unsatisfactory was this state of affairs. They decided to attempt an improvement, and, guided only by natural sympathy and unbounded faith in the virtue of handicrafts, they yet tackled the business more scientifically than the hospitals had done.

First, the malady being nervous, they insisted on cheerful environment. The room in Forster Square, large, well-ventilated, open to the light on three sides, was the best home for the club that could be found in the city. The men work at long trestle tables; cupboards are provided to store their pieces and the models they copy; and, for the rest, blue curtains against the yellow walls and a bowl or two of flowers make the room a delightful workshop.

Second, to give the men some incentive to work, all articles (except a man's first piece, which he is allowed to keep) are sold, and the maker is paid the difference between the selling price and the cost of materials.

Third, to give the public some incentive to buy, a certain standard of work must be maintained. At first this would seem to have little bearing on the treatment of shell-shock, but it is of vital importance to the life and work of the club. If no standard were set, the men, in moments of impatience or apathy, might become slipshod; the work would deteriorate in quality; it would lose its interest, and the men would finally throw it over in disgust. The teachers set a high standard at the beginning, and by long and earnest consultations on the relative values of knot and splice, of eight-plait and macramé cord, and by ceaseless experiment they have raised it considerably. The result is that there has been a demand for the work, and most of the men are now executing definite orders. The articles made by the club cost more than those sold in a shop, but as they show some marked improvement—a better finish or greater durability—they are worth the price put upon them. A string bag bought at a shop, for instance, is usually a subject of shame to the average shopper. Empty, she folds it up into the smallest possible compass and secretes it; full, she hastens home with it through little-frequented streets, her eyes downcast, hoping she will not be seen. A bag made at the club, however, with its fringes and tassels, its elegant shape and cunningly-wrought handles, may be carried proudly in the light of day before all men. It is an ornament!

THE CHOICE OF WORK.

Fourth, and most important of all, to interest the men in the work for its own sake, discretion must be shown in the choice of handicrafts. Robinson Crusoe, that most resourceful craftsman, explained the secret of his success, thus: "As reason is the substance and original of mathematics, so by stating and squaring everything by reason, and by making the most rational judgment of things, every man may be in time master of every mechanical art." And there is joy in thus exercising the reason and judgment; and there is satisfaction in contemplating the finished work, the labour of hand and brain. Herein lies all the charm and the virtue of handicrafts. There are certain mechanical arts, however, which yield the lazy satisfaction without the joy of exercising reason or judgment. Knitting is a good example, as Dickens showed in "A Tale of Two Cities," and it is obvious that a work in which the mind is free to count heads rolling into a sawdust basket is not suitable for a man suffering from a nervous complaint like shell-shock.

The teachers have striven to avoid these crafts and to discover those which occupy without puzzling the mind, and provide the greatest variety of interest. Adam Smith and his theory about division of labour are ignored. The advantages he urges in favour of his system—increased dexterity and saving of time—count for nothing. What is time to these men with the awful leisure of convalescents, deprived of books and unable to visit the theatre? Of what use is dexterity to those who cannot keep their limbs still? The one drawback to the system—that it makes work monotonous and mechanical—rules division of labour out finally. So a man nets his bag and makes the macramé fringes and tassels as well. Truly we are back in the middle ages.

Under this care and thought the club has prospered. The room on the floor above has been acquired; four weaving looms, two supplied by the Bradford Technical College and two by the Shipley education authorities, have been installed, and lessons are given twice a week. The doctors at the Abram Peel military hospital, sensible of the value of the club, have modified the rule that no man shall be allowed out in the morning, and grant early passes to all craftsmen. So the membership has grown, until now the register contains the names of nearly 200 men. They came to the club nervous wrecks, some hardly able to walk; they were put to work, netting, or weaving, or stitching, and the charm fell upon them. The brightness of the room, the atmosphere of busy contentment cheered them; the ordered methodical work soothed them; they became interested in the pattern growing daily under their hands, anxious to keep it perfect. The cure had begun.

Some of the men are still at the club, improving rapidly, others have been discharged from hospital and have left the club. For a brief space this peaceful haven of old-world industry was theirs; then out again into the turmoil and complexity of the twentieth century. Sic volvere Parcas. ... soldier, however, has learnt better than the ... man how to meet the Fates, be their decrees tender or cruel. He leaves his work without a sigh, without a boast to cover his regret, and goes out to face them, smiling, unafraid.

Newspaper cutting about rehabilitation centre in Bradford.
RAIL 491/854

The Committee drew up a questionnaire and called upon various witnesses. The questionnaire dealt with issues such as military training and recruitment, and the nature of shell shock. The questions were, perhaps unsurprisingly, based around military medicine and military matters. The witnesses themselves ranged from regiment and battalion commanders; to medical officers who had treated shell shock at home and at the Front; to Ministry of Pensions officials; to those men who had suffered from shell shock. All were connected directly with the issue of shell shock.

Their final report, which was published in 1922, contains excerpts from these witnesses, including Lord Gort, who was a senior British Army officer, and Colonel Burnett of the 1st Battalion Gordon Highlanders.

The final pages of it also contain a summary of the recommendations that the Committee reached. One of these related to terminology, in which they stated that the term shell shock should be removed from official parlance, and that the conditions which would normally fall under this heading should be called by their designated medical terms. Recommendations as to prevention were also put forward. For example, every possible means should be taken to promote morale, esprit de corps and a high standard of discipline, and that training should be prolonged until the man has had time to acquire the correct standard of morale to put the welfare of his unit before his own. When on duty, things like leave home and short tours of duty in the front line in stationary warfare, especially in bad sectors, were encouraged. Forms of treatment and return to the front lines are also discussed, which link into the case of Sassoon.

45

impossible for the person so afflicted to continue to face fire. This latter must be looked upon as a disgrace in an army which hopes to retain its efficiency. He said " the number of cases of " actual ' shell shock ' was very few, but of breakdown and " nerves, enormous—hundreds of them."

Asked whether in " shell shock " he considered that the neurasthenic condition played a part, the Colonel said he thought neurasthenia might be a result of it. In one case, in the battalion he commanded was a regular soldier with 12 years' service. He had been blown up by a shell early in the war. When he returned to the battalion in 1916 he was perfectly normal to talk to, but in the trenches as soon as a shell came over he was simply filled with terror and except for the fact that he was well known throughout the battalion he might have been infectious.

The Colonel said his battalion was drawn entirely from agricultural labourers. He also commanded a brigade of West Riding Territorials. The standard of *esprit de corps* in Regular battalions was always better than in Second Line Territorial battalions and the experience was that after sustaining casualties in action it was always harder to get second line battalions trained up again. He was quite certain that in a pre-war Regular battalion so long as the officer himself did not go back with a nervous breakdown, very few of the men would. The officer would not find that the whole of the platoon had gone back with a nervous breakdown and he was advancing by himself. In a modern battle he added there is always a procession of men left behind who remain in dug-outs and say they have been blown up by shells. A large proportion of them are so left because they do not want to go on. There was the case of a man on the Somme in 1916 who did not go over the top with the rest of the battalion. His story was that he was blown down the dug-out by a shell. He was unable to prove the story and was tried for his life and sentenced to be shot. The sentence was held over, but the next time he went into action he got recommended for a Distinguished Conduct Medal. That man had made a final effort to control himself and had recovered.

Asked whether he was of opinion that it was a disgrace to the man to lose control of his actions or a disgrace to the Army, Colonel Burnett replied, " A disgrace to the man. Although a " man's nerves may break down we must look upon it as a dis- " grace, otherwise you would have everybody breaking down as " soon as they wanted to go home. People who have not served " with regiments are sometimes apt to sneer at Colonel So-and- " so, who commanded a battalion for two years and then failed, " without making allowance for the strain which a long course " of battle experiences entails."

Colonel Burnett added that he went out in October, 1914, with the 2nd Battalion of the Gordons, and did not remember seeing anything of the sort, *i.e.,* " shell shock," among the regular soldiers.

Report of the War Office Committee of Enquiry into "Shell-shock". *WO 32/4748*

50

" was not ' shell shock ' as I understand it but they were worn
" out and finished."

Asked whether when Commanding Officers saw a man
obviously breaking down they sent him back to the Base, Lord
Gort said, " Yes, but it was a difficulty. If you once allowed
" people to go away you felt you were not playing the game to
" the Army." He added that he thought that it would be worth
while getting statistics of the incidence of " shell shock " in the
various divisions at different periods. He thought it would be
found that in first-class divisions there was practically no " shell
shock."*

Lord Gort added, " I think the whole question of training is
" one of morale and *esprit de corps* and that in face of strong
" morale and *esprit de corps* ' shell shock ' would be practically
" non-existent. Where there is a good battalion commander
" the men will always play up to him ; if he sets the example the
" rest will follow. In peace training the great thing is drill.
" No doubt you want something to help you over your fears
" and if you get control of the nerves, as you do in drill, it helps
" largely and it helps to drive the man forward in war. For an
" instance of that, the Canadians fell back on drill as an excellent
" way of improving the general morale of their divisions.
" Another form of morale raising is regimental history—to tell
" men of the deeds done by the regiment. The feeling of
" unionism—of moving together—is a great help and this is
" brought out by the soldiers' training—drill.

" Another most important point is that in France we put great
" store on drilling battalions every morning when they were out
" of the line. It made them move as a mass and undoubtedly
" created the feeling in them that they belonged to a body
" capable of moving as a whole and not as individuals."

Lord Gort added, " I think ' shell shock,' like measles, is so
" infectious that you cannot afford to run risks with it at all and
" in war the individual is of small account. If one or two go
" by the board it is extremely unfortunate and sad but it cannot
" be helped. A large proportion must be wounded or killed. It
" must be looked upon as a form of disgrace to the soldier. A
" certain class of men are all right out of the line, but the minute
" they know they are to go back they start getting ' shell shock '
" and so forth. If such a man had been in a bad condition it
" would have been seen by his Commanding Officer and he would
" have been examined by the Medical Officer and passed out of
" the line. Officers must be taught much more about man
" mastership in the same way as horse mastership. I
" think further care should be taken to teach commanders
" that at the Staff College, so that they do not overtax
" the men. It is all to a great extent a question of discipline

* *Note.*—The general evidence favours Lord Gort's opinion, but such statistics
are not available.

Report of the War Office Committee of Enquiry into "Shell-shock". *WO 32/4748*

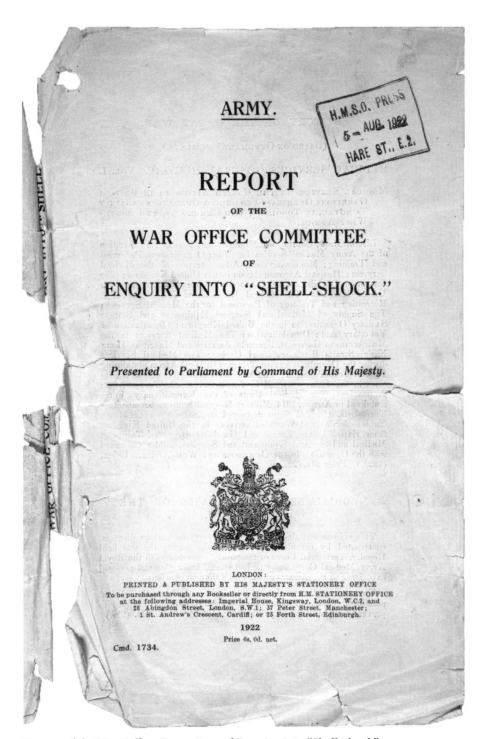

ARMY.

REPORT

OF THE

WAR OFFICE COMMITTEE

OF

ENQUIRY INTO "SHELL-SHOCK."

Presented to Parliament by Command of His Majesty.

LONDON:
PRINTED & PUBLISHED BY HIS MAJESTY'S STATIONERY OFFICE
To be purchased through any Bookseller or directly from H.M. STATIONERY OFFICE
at the following addresses: Imperial House, Kingsway, London, W.C.2, and
28 Abingdon Street, London, S.W.1; 37 Peter Street, Manchester;
1 St. Andrew's Crescent, Cardiff; or 23 Forth Street, Edinburgh.

1922

Price 6s. 0d. net.

Cmd. 1734.

Report of the War Office Committee of Enquiry into "Shell-shock". *WO 32/4748*

190

(3) Psychiatry;
(4) Psychopathology, including the nature and treatment of the various types of psychoneurosis, and the doctrines and relationships of the various schools of thought.
(5) Clinical instruction.

It would seem to be very desirable that a limited number of R.A.M.C. officers should undergo a complete course of instruction of this type so that suitable centres of treatment can be rapidly organised on the outbreak of war.

The recommendations of the Committee may be summarised as follows :— SUMMARY OF RECOMMENDATIONS

Large Caps
delete A /

I.—General.

1. The term shell-shock should be eliminated from official nomenclature, the disorders hitherto included under this heading being designated by the recognised medical terms for such conditions. Abbreviations such as N.Y.D. Nervous or Mental, or N.Y.D.N., D.A.H., etc., should be avoided, as they are liable to become catchwords, and so react unfavourably on the patients themselves and on others.

Classification of Casualties.

1. Concussion or commotion attended by loss of consciousness and evidence of organic lesion of the central nervous system or its adjacent organs (such as rupture of the membrana tympani) should be classified as a battle casualty.

2. No case of psycho-neurosis or of mental breakdown, even when attributed to a shell explosion or the effects thereof, should be classified as a battle casualty any more than sickness or disease is so regarded.

3. In all doubtful cases it is desirable to have the classification determined by a Board of expert Medical Officers after observation in a neurological hospital.

Prevention.

1. (A) *Training.*—Every possible means should be taken to promote morale, esprit de corps and a high standard of discipline.

2. Training should be sufficiently prolonged to ensure that the soldier is not only physically fit and efficient, but also that he has had time to acquire such a standard of morale as will enable him to put the welfare of his unit before his own personal safety.

3. Close observation should be made by officers, both regimental and medical, and by non-commissioned officers of the unit on individuals during the whole of their training, so that abnormalities from which mental or nervous instability may be inferred may not be overlooked. For this purpose there should be the frankest co-operation between regimental and medical officers.

Report of the War Office Committee of Enquiry into "Shell-shock". *WO 32/4748*

191

4. The study of character, so far as it is applicable to military life, is recommended for all officers with a view to teaching Man-Mastership.

5. Special instruction should be given to Royal Army Medical Corps officers in the psycho-neurosis and psychoses as they occur in war; and selected officers should be encouraged to specialise in the study of these disorders.

 (B) *On Active Service.*—The practice of withdrawal of officers and men showing incipient signs of nervous breakdown or over-fatigue for rest either in the battalion or divisional area should be officially recognised and systematised.

2. So far as the military situation permits, tours of duty in the front line in stationary warfare should be short, especially in bad sectors. Adequate rest and organised recreation should be provided for units when out of the line.

3. Monotony should be avoided by changing units, as circumstances permit, between fronts and sectors.

Leave home should be encouraged.

4. The promotion of all measures making for good sanitation and the physical comfort of the men, both in the line and also in rest billets and base depots, should receive constant attention.

5. Rest of mind and body is essential in all cases showing signs of incipient nervous breakdown, and when possible it should be given under conditions of security and comfort and freedom from all military duties.

6. The fullest use should be made of Convalescent Depots for re-training and hardening men discharged from hospital. These units should invariably be pervaded by an atmosphere of complete cure.

The above recommendations, suitably modified to meet particular circumstances, should be applied to the other fighting services.

Treatment.

(A) *In Forward Areas.*—No soldier should be allowed to think that loss of nervous or mental control provides an honourable avenue of escape from the battlefield, and every endeavour should be made to prevent slight cases leaving the battalion or divisional area, where treatment should be confined to provision of rest and comfort for those who need it and to heartening them for return to the front line.

(B) *In Neurological Centres.*—When cases are sufficiently severe to necessitate more scientific and elaborate treatment they should be sent to special Neurological Centres as near the front as possible, to be under the care of an expert in nervous disorders. No such case should, however, be so labelled on evacuation as to fix the idea of nervous breakdown in the patient's mind.

(C) *In Base Hospitals.*—When evacuation to the base is necessary, cases should be treated in a separate hospital or in separate sections of a hospital, and not with the ordinary sick and

Report of the War Office Committee of Enquiry into "Shell-shock". *WO 32/4748*

192

wounded patients. Only in exceptional circumstances should cases be sent to the United Kingdom, as, for instance, men likely to be unfit for further service of any kind with the forces in the field. This policy should be widely known throughout the Force.

Forms of Treatment.

The establishment of an atmosphere of cure is the basis of all successful treatment, the personality of the physician is, therefore, of the greatest importance. While recognising that each individual case of war neurosis must be treated on its merits, the Committee are of opinion that good results will be obtained in the majority by the simplest forms of psycho-therapy, *i.e.*, explanation, persuasion and suggestion, aided by such physical methods as baths, electricity and massage, though these act chiefly by suggestion. Rest of mind and body is essential in all cases.

The Committee are of opinion that the production of the hypnoidal state and deep hypnotic sleep, while beneficial as a means of conveying suggestions or eliciting forgotten experiences are useful in selected cases, but in the majority they are unnecessary and may even aggravate the symptoms for a time.

They do not recommend psycho-analysis in the Freudian sense.

In the state of convalescence, re-education and suitable occupation of an interesting nature are of great importance. If the patient is unfit for further military service, it is considered that every endeavour should be made to obtain for him suitable employment on his return to active life.

Return to the Fighting Line.

Soldiers should not be returned to the fighting line under the following conditions :—

(1) If the symptoms of neurosis are of such a character that the soldier cannot be treated overseas with a view to subsequent useful employment.
(2) If the breakdown is of such severity as to necessitate a long period of rest and treatment in the United Kingdom.
(3) If the disability is anxiety neurosis of a severe type.
(4) If the disability is a mental breakdown or psychosis requiring treatment in a mental hospital.

It is, however, considered that many of such cases could, after recovery, be usefully employed in some form of auxiliary military duty.

Cowardice, Desertion and Neurosis.

In many cases it is extremely difficult to distinguish cowardice from neurosis since in both fear is the chief causal

Report of the War Office Committee of Enquiry into "Shell-shock". *WO 32/4748*

193

factor. The Committee recommend that the system pursued in France in the late war, of obtaining the best possible expert advice when any medical question or doubt arose, before or at trials for serious military offences, or on subsequent review of the proceedings of the Court, should be followed in the future.

Recruiting.

1. Every effort should be made at the time of enlistment to ascertain the nervous and mental conditions of candidates both from their previous histories and from their present condition.

2. Only " fit " men as judged by the pre-war standards for the regular Army should be enlisted into the regu... is desirable to accept men falling into Grade II or III or Ministry of National Service for the Militia or Territorial Army, they should be re-graded (with those accepted for Grade I) every year.

3. All Regular, Special Reserve and Territorial Force Medical Officers should undergo a prescribed course of instruction in the methods of examination of recruits and the physical and mental standards required. Special officers should be earmarked in each district for these duties on mobilization. In addition, a selection should be made from those who served with His Majesty's Forces or were employed as civilians on the examination of recruits during 1914-18, and a separate list kept of those selected.

4. On mobilization the recruiting machinery should be expanded on the lines indicated above, and measures should be taken to see that recruits receive an adequate medical examination. As soon as possible Medical Boards should take the place of single recruiting medical officers.

5. The allocation of recruits to suitable military units should be the function of Posting Boards advised by special medical officers.

6. If military service is made compulsory the procedure employed by the Ministry of National Service for the medical examination and grading of recruits should be put into operation.

In conclusion the Committee desire to record their sorrow at the loss they sustained by the death of their friend and colleague, Dr. H. W. Kaye, of the Medical Directorate of the Ministry of Pensions. Throughout their long deliberations, he gave them his generous and whole-hearted support; and his experience in regard to matters important to the enquiry was always influenced by the kindly interest he felt for those who had suffered in mind or in body as a consequence of the War. They feel that by his untimely death a valuable life has been lost to the service of the country.

Report of the War Office Committee of Enquiry into "Shell-shock". *WO 32/4748*

CHAPTER 5

PEACE DAY

The Peace Day celebrations of July 1919 were to be organised by the Cabinet Peace Celebrations Committee, under the presidency of Lord Curzon. They would discuss all matters in connection with the ceremonies and would deal with all the details such as the routes for processions; the arrangements for military and police; pageants; firework displays; etc. They would also work with the Office of Works. The duties of this Office were as follows: the erection of all stands, as well as the allocation of seats thereon and the issue of all tickets for them; photography and cinematography; press; ambulances; sanitary arrangements; fire; police; drinking water; attendants; stewards; bandstands; camps; decorations; illuminations; trees planted in celebration of peace; and the giving out of police passes to officers and workmen on duty.

The Committee met for the first time on 9 May 1919, where they outlined the form that these celebrations of peace could take. At their meeting a month later, they had received some feedback from the Prime Minister, who had spoken to the French government to see how they would be celebrating. They replied that there would be no organised celebrations, and that the signing of peace would be celebrated by a military display only. At the meeting of the War Cabinet on the same morning, there had been absolute concurrence in the view that it would be impossible in Great Britain to limit the festivities to a Military Parade immediately following the German signature. It had also been pointed out that these celebrations should not just involve the Army, in particular with the First Lord of the Admiralty expressing opinion that the public would wish to see the Navy involved. All of this led the War Office to believe that nothing grand would be able to be organised in the few days surrounding the signing at Versailles – especially as that was not long after the meeting where all of this was discussed. The point of these festivities was to involve everyone. It was to be a popular celebration, and not just something that was enjoyed by the wealthier classes.

The question of whether female war workers should be included in the military display in London was brought up at one of these meetings. The Chairman thought that the public would generally expect to see representatives of bodies such as the YMCA, the Red Cross

Victory Parade, London. *WORK 21/74*

Victory Parade, London. *WORK 21/74*

Victory Parade, London. *WORK 21/74*

and St. John's Ambulance, the WRAF, WAAC and WRNS. It was decided that representatives from the above bodies should be invited to participate, and that the total number of women in the procession should not exceed 1,500.[1]

The National Peace Celebrations of July 1919 had lots going on. In the morning there was a procession which starting at the Albert Gate at 10am, took in a route which covered the west and south of the city, before finishing at Hyde Park Corner at 12.20pm.[2] The order of the procession was as follows: representatives of the Allied forces; United States of America (including General Pershing); Belgium; China; Czechoslovakia; France (including Foch); Greece; Italy; Japan; Poland; Portugal; Romania; Serbia and Siam. Then came representatives of the forces of the British Empire: Naval section – including Queen Alexandra's Royal Naval Nursing Service and the WRNS; the Army – including Haig and representatives from everyone from the Yeomanry to the Infantry. Also included in this section were the Indian Army, the Royal Army Service Corps, the Royal Army Medical Corps, the various nursing groups, the Indian Army Nurses, chaplains, and the QMAAC; and finally the Royal Air Force – including chaplains and medical services, and the Women's Royal Air Force.[3]

Victory Parade, London. *WORK 21/74*

Victory Parade, London. *WORK 21/74*

Victory Parade, London. *WORK 21/74*

Victory Parade, London. *WORK 21/74*

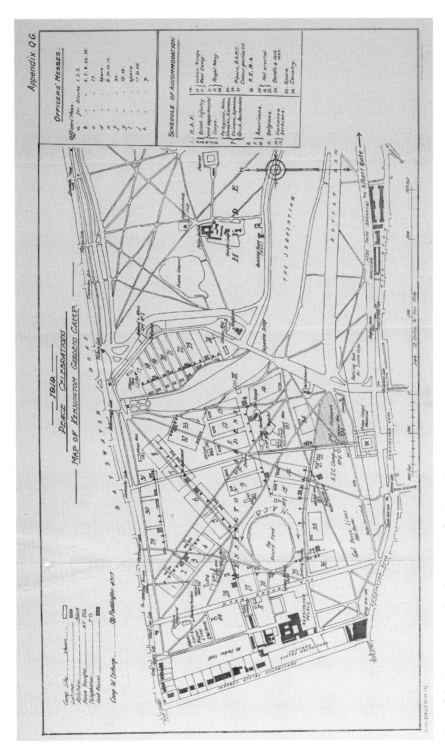

Map of the Kensington Gardens camp for Peace Day. *WORK 21/74*

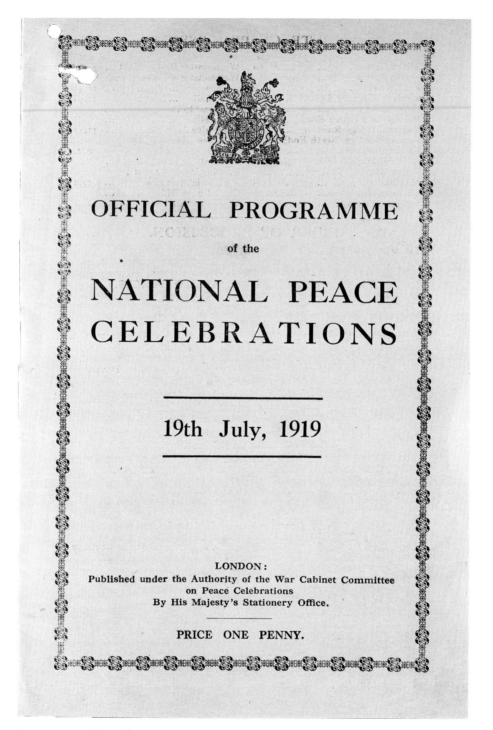

OFFICIAL PROGRAMME

of the

NATIONAL PEACE CELEBRATIONS

19th July, 1919

LONDON:
Published under the Authority of the War Cabinet Committee
on Peace Celebrations
By His Majesty's Stationery Office.

PRICE ONE PENNY.

Front cover of the official programme for the Peace Day celebrations. *WORK 21/74*

The celebrations were to be as inclusive as possible. This was further proven by a whole programme of children's festivities held in the afternoon in various royal parks.

Activities ranged from concerts and country dancing to storytelling and ballet performances. There was also a concert in the evening by the Imperial Choir of Peace and Thanksgiving, and the Massed Bands of the Brigade of Guards.

At 9.45pm there was further entertainment for all to enjoy, with a firework display; the programme for which showed 84 different parts to it.[4] At 11pm, and the final thing on the programme, it was organised that Admiralty deck flares would be lit in Hyde Park, St. James's Park, Regent's Park, Greenwich Park, Hampstead Heath, Finsbury Park, Victoria Park, Southwark Park, Kennington Park, Battersea Park, Streatham Common, Meath Gardens, Wormwood Scrubs, Epsom Downs, Harrow-on-the-Hill, Putney Heath, Richmond Bus Station, and Crystal Palace. These flares were estimated to burn for around 15 minutes.

Seating had been a concern for members of the Committee, especially how to erect enough for everyone and in places where the view would be worthwhile. Members of both Houses of Parliament were accommodated on stands at the south side of the Mall. Wounded officers and men were positioned on the terraces opposite the Queen Victoria Memorial and on a stand on the south side of the Mall. Chelsea and Greenwich Pensioners had seats at the end of the Mall, near the Queen Victoria Memorial. Children from the

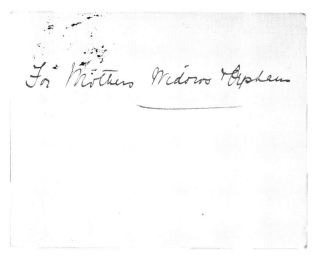

Front and back of ticket for the celebrations. *WORK 21/74*

BUCKINGHAM PALACE

8th July 1919.

My dear Lionel,

The Queen desires me to tell you that Her
Majesty has from time to time received requests that
the claims of widows,mothers,daughters,&c. of sailors
and soldiers should not be forgotten in any arrangements
which may be contemplated in connection with stands
for viewing the various processions on the 19th instant
or on other days.

The Queen would like to think that these poor
women will not be forgotten.   Even if it is not possible
to accommodate large numbers, Her Majesty thought it
just worth while to remind you of the matter.

Yours ever,

Harry L Verney.

Sir Lionel Earle,K.C.B. C.M.G.
        Secretary,
            H.M.Office of Works,
                Storey's Gate, S.W.1.

Letter from the Queen regarding making space for women in the spectators' area. *WORK 21/74*

Victory Parade, London. *WORK 21/74*

Service Orphan Homes had a stand on the west side of Constitution Hill. Discharged soldiers and sailors had a reserved spot on the Mall, in between Marlborough Gate and the Duke of York steps. On the suggestion of the Queen, the Green Park side of Constitution Hill was reserved for widows, mothers and orphans of officers and men who fell in the war. The total number of tickets issued for the event was 27, 283.[5]

On 25 July, another letter was sent saying that the Queen had received many charming and grateful letters from poor women who 'had enjoyed splendid views of the Procession on Saturday 19 July from part of the Park near Constitution Hill which had been set aside for them by the Office of Works.'[6] The Queen wished to pass on her thanks for the pleasure that this department had made possible for these spectators, and to acknowledge the extremely hard work that had gone into dealing with the innumerable applications and in allotting and arranging places in that part of the park for them. It finished with the following sentiment:

> 'Her Majesty would be glad, should you think it right to do so, if you would convey to all concerned an expression of Her Majesty's sincere appreciation of their successful

efforts to render Saturday last a day long to be remembered by those in whose welfare The Queen was particularly interested'.[7]

Arrangements were also made with the Ministry of Food to have marquees set up at various points along the main route. These marquees had supplies of things such as lemonade and ginger beer, as well as cakes and scones. Ham and corned beef was also supplied for making sandwiches. A letter from the Director of Kitchens at the Ministry of Food, two days after the event, stated that the public and press alike were singing the praises of these marquees. They were very popular, and the prices were reasonable. Over 120,000 people were served and the total takings amounted to £1,400.[8]

Further celebrations were planned for the start of August 1919. On 2 August there was a march of the Indian Army and those attached. On 4 August a river procession, organised by the Admiralty, included not just the Navy but also those such as the Mercantile Marines.

CHAPTER 6

THE UNKNOWN WARRIOR

At the west end of the nave in Westminster Abbey lies the grave of the Unknown Warrior, an unidentified British soldier killed on a European battlefield during the First World War, who was buried here on 11 November 1920. Simultaneously, in France, the similar internment of an unidentified French soldier occurred at the Arc de Triomphe. The grave at Westminster, which contains soil from the battlefields, an idea suggested by the Dean of Westminster, is covered with a slab of black Belgian marble, from a quarry near Namur.[1] On this marble is inscribed the following, composed by Herbert Edward Ryle, the Dean of Westminster:

'Beneath this stone rests the body
of a British warrior
unknown by name or rank
brought from France to lie among
the most illustrious of the land
and buried here on Armistice Day
11 Nov: 1920, in the presence of
His Majesty King George V
His Ministers of State
the Chiefs of His Forces
and a vast concourse of the Nation

Thus are commemorated the many
multitudes who during the Great
War of 1914-1914 gave the most that
man can give life itself
for God
for King and Country
for loved ones home and empire
for the sacred cause of justice and
the freedom of the world

They buried him among the Kings because he
had done good toward God and toward
His house'[2]

Around the main inscription are four other pieces of text, taken from the New Testament:

'The Lord knoweth them that are His'
'Greater love hath no man than this'
'Unknown and yet well known, dying and behold we live'
'In Christ shall all be made alive'[3]

The idea for this burial seems to have first come from the Reverend David Railton, who became a chaplain to the 2nd battalion of the Honourable Artillery Company during the war. In 1916, in a back garden near Armentieres, he noticed a grave with a rough cross to mark the spot. On the cross were pencilled the words: 'An Unknown British Soldier'. After the war, he became a vicar in Margate. In 1920, he wrote to Herbert Ryle suggesting that a permanent memorial to the fallen who had no known grave should be erected.

On the night of 7 November 1920, suitable remains were brought to the chapel at St Pol, near Arras. Accounts say sometimes four bodies, sometimes six, but these were chosen from the battlefields of Ypres, Arras, the Somme and the Aisne; the bodies being mere bones, which were beyond all recognition.[4] The General Officer in charge of troops in France and Flanders, Brigadier General L.J. Wyatt, and Lieutenant Colonel Gell of the Directorate of Graves Registration and Enquiries, went into the chapel alone. The bodies were laid out on stretchers, covered with a Union Jack, with no way of telling which body came from which battlefield. General Wyatt chose a body, and this was placed into a plain coffin, which was then sealed. The other bodies were taken away for reburial. At noon, a joint ceremony was held over the coffin, which was then taken by ambulance to Boulogne, where a temporary chapel had been erected. The body lay under the guard of a company of the French 8th Infantry Battalion until the morning of 10 November, when two British undertakers arrived. They placed the body in a heavy coffin made from oak wood from Hampton Court, banded with iron work.[5] Plans for the coffin which held this man have the inscription shield attached saying the following:

'A British warrior
who fell in the Great
War of 1914-1918 for
King and empire'[6]

Allied graves at Green Hill cemetery, Gallipoli. *WO 32/5640*

Allied graves at Redoubt cemetery, Gallipoli. *WO 32/5640*

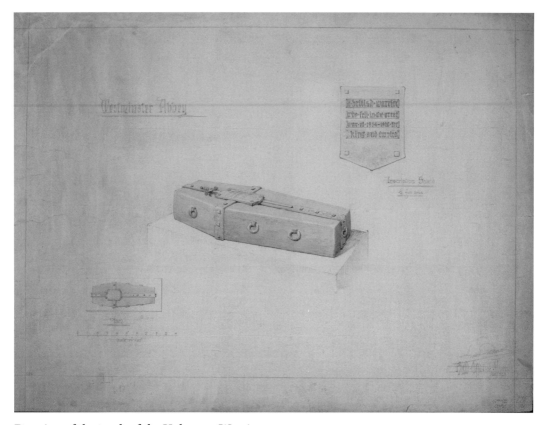

Drawing of the tomb of the Unknown Warrior. *WORK 31/2252*

The original idea was for the inscription to say 'country' instead of 'empire'. However, the Committee who were in charge of these plans strongly desired that this change be made, and clearly this wish was adhered to.

At 10.30 am on the 10th, all the bells of Boulogne rang out and the coffin containing the Unknown Warrior was escorted to the Quai Gambetta, where Marshal Foch and HMS Verdun were waiting. An hour later, the ship and her precious cargo began the journey to Dover. The official plans for the journey afterwards were as follows – the coffin would be brought to Victoria station by a special saloon carriage, where it would be placed under the guard of the 1st Battalion Grenadier Guards.[7] This is how it would remain until the following morning.

On the morning of 11 November, the day of the interment of the Unknown Warrior, the Firing Party was to consist of one Sergeant, one Corporal and twelve Guardsmen of the 3rd Battalion Coldstream Guards. The Gun Carriage had a team of six horses, and was furnished by 'N' Battery of the Royal Horse Artillery. It was on to this carriage that the coffin was laid, draped in a flag. The Bearers were another party comprised of members of the Coldstream

Guards. One of the most important decisions was that the Pall Bearers would be made up of twelve Distinguished Officers of the Royal Navy, the Army, and the Royal Air Force – in order to give representation to all the forces. The accompanying bands were comprised of: the bands and drums of the Coldstream Guards, the Scots Guards, the Irish Guards and the Welsh Guards; as well as the pipes of the Scots Guards. 828 mourners from all ranks of the Royal Navy, Army and Royal Air Force were to accompany the coffin as it made its way to Westminster; along with 400 representatives from various ex-servicemen's organisations.[8] Everything was planned out meticulously by the Committee.

At 9.40am, the Firing Party began to move off, to the sounds of the bands beginning to play, whilst the Royal Horse Artillery began to fire a salute of 19 Minute Guns in Hyde Park.[9] The bands were to play continuously throughout the march. The Gun Carriage, escorted by the Pall Bearers, and followed by the Bearers, marched behind the bands. The Mourners would follow behind, with the ex-servicemen following them. The route took them towards Constitution Hill, then eastwards along the Mall, through Admiralty Arch

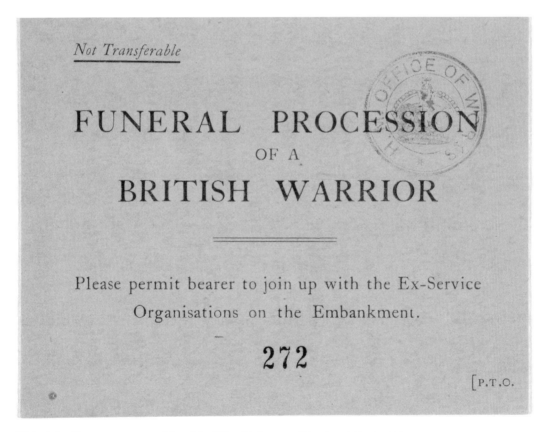

Ticket for the ceremony and burial of the Unknown Warrior. *WORK 20/1/3*

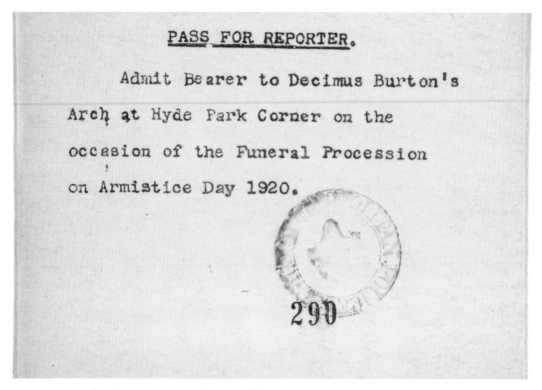

Reporter pass for the ceremony and burial of the Unknown Warrior. *WORK 20/1/3*

into Trafalgar Square and Whitehall, where the King, the Royal Family and the leaders of the country were waiting at the Cenotaph. After the dedication of the Cenotaph, and a two minutes silence, the procession began the last short part of its journey – to Westminster, and the nave at the west end, where the Unknown Warrior was to have his place.

A shortened form of the Burial Service took place inside, beginning with the singing of the verses 'I am the resurrection and the life' and 'Though knowest Lord' during the procession to the grave. The coffin was brought to the west nave through the congregation of mourners, and a guard of honour of 100 holders of the Victoria Cross. The King dropped a handful of the earth from the battlefields onto the coffin, as it was lowered into the grave. Servicemen kept watch at each of the four corners of the grave, as thousands of mourners moved past. The guard of honour remained there constantly, watching over the Unknown Warrior. The grave was finally filled in, using earth from the battlefields, on 18 November.[10] The current black marble stone was presented at a special service a year following. The important factor about this Unknown Warrior is that he could be from any of the three services: Army, Royal Navy or Royal Air Force and from any part of the British Isles or Empire, and can therefore represent all of those who died who have no other marked memorial or grave.

CHAPTER 7

THE CENOTAPH

The Cenotaph, positioned in Whitehall, has become the central focus of remembrance and for commemoration events in Britain since the First World War. Designed by Sir Edwin Lutyens, it was first unveiled on 19 July 1919, for the Peace Day parade.

Before the end of the war, Lutyens was appointed one of three principal architects for the Imperial War Graves Commission, now the Commonwealth War Graves Commission. He was involved in many monuments to commemorate the dead. Larger cemeteries have a Stone of Remembrance in them, which was designed by him. Apart from the Cenotaph, the next most well-known of his memorials is probably the Memorial to the Missing of the Somme, at Thiepval.

The first iteration of the Cenotaph came when Lloyd George expressed a desire to see something akin to the catafalque which had been built beside the Arc de Triomphe. He wanted a temporary structure which would honour the war dead. This would end up being one of a number of temporary structures erected for the Peace Day parade. The request for this monument came only two weeks before the celebration, and Lloyd George approached Lutyens about being the architect of it. It was Lutyens who believed that the design should represent more the Cenotaph than the catafalque suggested by Lloyd George. Lutyens referred to it more as a Cenotaph to convey the simple meaning of 'an empty tomb up-lifted on high pedestal.'[1] Originally built from wood and plaster, the Cenotaph became the place where troops gave a salute as they marched past, on 19 July. It became one of the central images from that day.

A letter from the First Commissioner of Works, dated two days after the Peace Day celebrations stated the following:

'It has been decided to allow the Memorial to the Dead in Whitehall to remain in position for another week at least as a very general desire from the public to that effect has been expressed. Many people will be coming from the country to see it as the outward symbol of the nation's gratitude to its sons who have made the great sacrifice.'[2]

THE ILLUSTRATED LONDON NEWS, JUNE 23, 1923.—1091

TO SHINE UPWARD WITH PERPETUAL LIGHT? THE CENOTAPH.

PHOTOGRAPH SPECIALLY TAKEN FOR "THE ILLUSTRATED LONDON NEWS."

SHOWING THE STONE WREATH ON THE TOP, WITHIN WHICH IT IS PROPOSED TO PLACE AN EVER-BURNING LIGHT : THE CENOTAPH : AND THE SURROUNDING ROADWAY TO BE PAVED WITH RUBBER FOR SILENCING THE NOISE OF TRAFFIC.

It was suggested recently by a group of M.P.'s, in a letter to the "Times," that "a fixed light, which would shine upward day and night," from the top of the Cenotaph in Whitehall, would add to its symbolic beauty. "No change," they wrote, "should be made in the appearance of the Cenotaph; nothing to mar its simple dignity ; all that is needed is that within the wreath on the upper surface there be fixed a circle of electric light. The light should burn always, and, though invisible by day, it would through dusk and darkness bear its message of enduring memory to the skies. We understand that it is purposed shortly to cover the roadway surrounding the Cenotaph with rubber, so that traffic itself, in passing, may be hushed ; and the occasion seems favourable to carry out what we have ventured to suggest." The writers also urged that the practice of saluting the Cenotaph should be invariable. The symbolism of a perpetual light, or altar fire, has been used both in Christianity and other religions, as among the Vestals of ancient Rome. A secular example from antiquity was the ever-burning light on the famous Pharos at Alexandria, the prototype of lighthouses. A modern parallel is afforded by the Toc H. Lamps of Maintenance.

Cenotaph. *WORK 20/139*

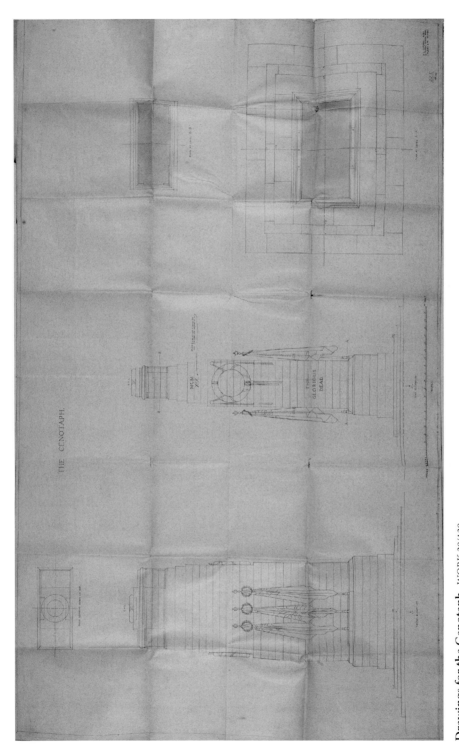

Drawings for the Cenotaph. *WORK 20/139*

A further letter dated 23 July introduced the idea that a great deal of public interest was being shown concerning the question of whether this temporary structure could be replaced by something permanent, either on its current site, or elsewhere.[3] A number of questions had already been raised to the Office of Works about this, and the press seemed to be in favour of it, also. Lutyens himself had written on the subject, too, urging making the memorial a permanent one on its present site, and expressing his readiness to design one on the same lines, with more elaboration than time had permitted with the temporary one. Pros and cons were made with regards to keeping it on the same site.

The pros were as follows:

1) It would be the historic spot where the Allied troops saluted the 'Glorious Dead' on Peace Day, and no other site would have the same historical and sentimental associations.

2) The monument itself was dignified and simple, and the position was a good and central one.

3) The public had become accustomed to seeing the monument on the present site, and the present design had received a considerable amount of public approval.

4) The erection of a monument along these lines on a permanent form would solve the question of a war memorial, which was surely soon to become a subject of public interest.

The considerations against keeping the permanent Cenotaph on this site were:

1) It could be argued that the position of such a monument in the middle of such a busy thoroughfare would likely obstruct traffic, in an area where it was already congested.

2) Although this monument was appropriate for the occasion, there was worry that it may not be regarded as sufficiently important, and could be seen as too mournful in character as a permanent expression of the triumphant victory of their arms.

3) There would probably be demand for a greater and more imposing memorial to be erected.

4) On the current site, it was likely to become habit, as in other cases, for the public to surround the Cenotaph with flowers and wreaths. This would be very difficult to control at the site on Whitehall, and could develop into unseemly untidiness.

5) The site was on ground which was under the control of the Westminster Borough Council, and permission from them would have to be obtained.

Cenotaph. *WORK 20/139*

The proposal to erect a replica of the current temporary design on some other site seemed scarcely worthy of consideration. It was deemed then that the whole point would be lost, and the Cenotaph itself would lose its appropriateness, having been designed for a special position and for a special occasion.[4] The London Traffic Advisory Committee, however, worried that a serious obstacle to the flow of traffic in so busy a main thoroughfare would cause accidents. They strongly recommended that it be moved to the centre of Parliament Square, where it could be flanked by the Houses of Parliament and Westminster Abbey. They viewed this suggested position as being less dangerous for people visiting the Cenotaph, but that it would also have the advantage of having more deeply grounded historical associations.

However, by 19 December, the House of Commons had voted with regards to the money required for the re-erection of the Cenotaph on its present site. The Financial Secretary to the Treasury had made a special point of this and, except for one member, no opposition was raised. From notices in the newspapers, it seemed that the decision for the new Cenotaph to be on the same site was what the public wanted. It was also believed that any reversal of the decision to have the new Cenotaph here would raise the question of design, as this monument had been specifically designed for the Whitehall site.

Questions were also raised as to changes in design and the features of the Cenotaph. The use of dyed and carved Portland stone to reproduce the national flags which decorate the Cenotaph was considered. Lutyens himself had been willing to trial this. In fact, in November 1919, he had involved the acclaimed sculptor Francis Derwent Wood in sculpting some examples of how these flags would look in stone. Lutyens believed that real flags would only make sense if the wreaths and other decorations were to also be real. However, the Cabinet insisted that real flags be used. It was urged that the use of stone was aesthetically objectionable and would weaken the emotional appeal of the memorial.[5] The estimated annual cost of renewable silk flags, which were the preferred option, was around £40.[6]

Speaking after its completion, Lutyens described the decision, by the sentiment of millions, that the Cenotaph remain as it was as 'no greater honour, no more complete and lasting satisfaction'.[7] Something else which remained unchanged was the inscription of 'The Glorious Dead' from his initial sketches. Suggestions were made for the changing of this inscription; including one from Prebendary Carlile, of the Church Army, who suggested, 'The souls of the righteous are in the Hand of God.'[8] All of these showed the desire to try and pay homage through words. But Lutyens was trying to convey the loss of all the people, from the Empire, with different denominations, who fought and died in the war. And a simple inscription was what he deemed the best manner in which to do so.

In this same text, Lutyens also mentions the change from stone flags to real ones. The reasons he gives for the flags being real are more poetic than one got from the Cabinet.

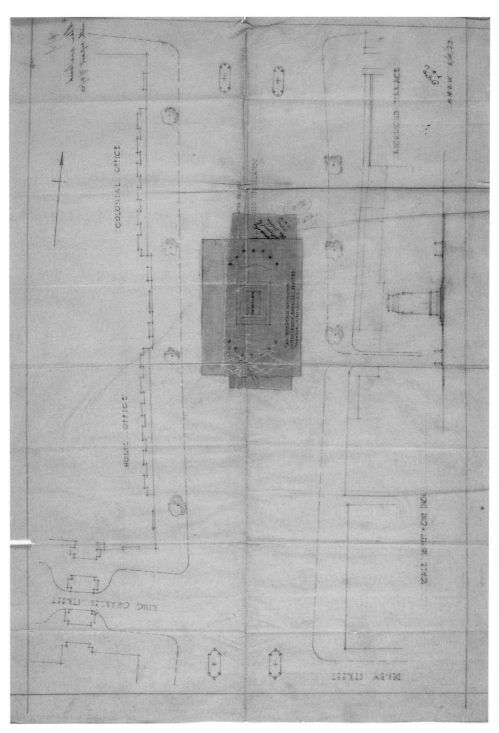

Further drawings of the site of the Cenotaph. *WORK 20/139*

SUGGESTED INSCRIPTIONS FOR

THE PERMANENT CENOTAPH IN WHITEHALL.

The Right Revd. The Lord Bishop of Winchester
(Acting for the Archbishop of Canterbury).

1.

Two inscriptions on opposite faces of the Memorial.

(1))Front)   "They loved not their lives unto the
                    death". (Rev.XII ii.)

(2) (Back)   "Fear not; I am He that liveth and was
                dead, and behold, I am alive for evermore".
                    (Rev. I. 17,18).

(This suggestion is tentative).

Mrs. Rimmer, Grey House, Queen's Drive, Mossley Hill, Liverpool.

2.

"Oh! ye who mourn in ceaseless pain,
        Be comforted.
They died for England; lives their name,
Emblazoned on the scroll of fame".

Barry J. Pole, 63, Overstone Road, W.6.

"They've gone, but still a memory held dear
By those who've lost remains. The battle's won
And those who lived through that great Hellish
                                        sphere
Return triumphant.But the men who've done
As much, and died a soldier's death "out there",
We cannot thank except by humble prayer.
So one and all we thank you for your share,
And ever will remember - you were men".

———————

"T'is scarcely understood how, in your prime,
The sacrifice you made to save the name,
Of England, and you've won in Foreign clime,
A wooden cross, and man's eternal fame.
But now a grateful nation does its best
To understand endurance at the test,
And prays to God your noble soul may rest
In everlasting peace henceforth - Amen".

———————

Suggested inscriptions for the Cenotaph. *WORK 20/139*

2.

Charles Dalmon, Esq.,
        18, Woburn Buildings, Upper Woburn Place, W.C.1.

        "The clods of battle-fields are red
        With Immortality; the Dead
        In their magnificence arise
        To shine before us through the skies".

Prebendary Carlile, D.D.,
        The Church Army, 55, Bryanston Street, Marble Arch, W.I.

        Suggests some inscription of a Christian
        nature, e.g.

        "The Souls of the Righteous are in the hand of
                        God". (Wisdom Q I.13.).

Alfred J. Green, Esq.,
        Vickers House, Broadway, Westminster.

    (A) "This simple stone proclaims from age to age,
        Their triumph is the whole world's heritage".

    (B) "They held the seas, they saved the lands; our all:
        Honour them, praise them, salute them withal".

    (C) "Their supreme sacrifice preserved for the world
        Freedom's Heritage".

    (D) "Ambassadors of Freedom's just renown,
        They for a common cause their lives laid down".

    (E) "When Darkness falls we forget not thee,
        Dawn breaks, and thou are still remembered".

    (F) "Like wheat that is sown they fell and died,
        Nor death immortal fame to them denied".

    (G) "They live in name and fame, though not in life".

Suggested inscriptions for the Cenotaph. *WORK 20/139*

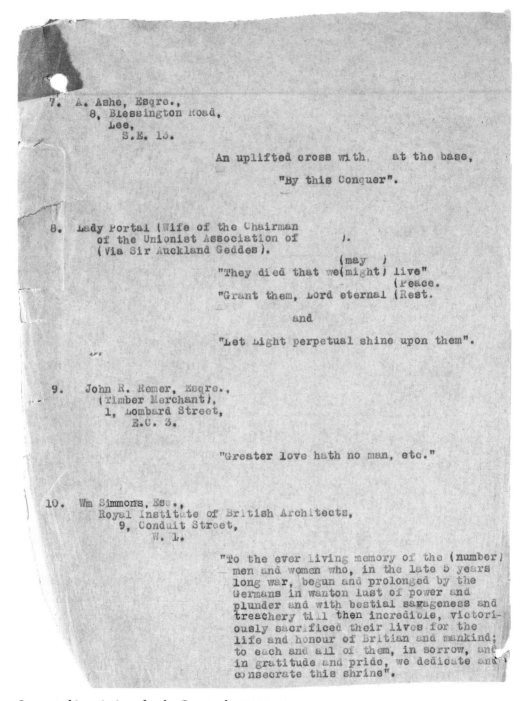

7. A. Ashe, Esqre.,
    8, Blessington Road,
       Lee,
          S.E. 13.

                    An uplifted cross with, at the base,

                            "By this Conquer".

8. Lady Portal (Wife of the Chairman
       of the Unionist Association of   ).
    (Via Sir Auckland Geddes).
                                        (may)
                    "They died that we(might) live"
                                                (Peace.
                    "Grant them, Lord eternal (Rest.

                            and

                    "Let Light perpetual shine upon them".

9. John R. Remer, Esqre.,
    (Timber Merchant),
       1, Lombard Street,
          E.C. 3.

                    "Greater love hath no man, etc."

10. Wm Simmons, Esq.,
       Royal Institute of British Architects,
          9, Conduit Street,
             W. 1.

                    "To the ever living memory of the (number)
                    men and women who, in the late 5 years
                    long war, begun and prolonged by the
                    Germans in wanton lust of power and
                    plunder and with bestial savageness and
                    treachery till then incredible, victori-
                    ously sacrificed their lives for the
                    life and honour of Britian and mankind;
                    to each and all of them, in sorrow, and
                    in gratitude and pride, we dedicate and
                    consecrate this shrine".

Suggested inscriptions for the Cenotaph. *WORK 20/139*

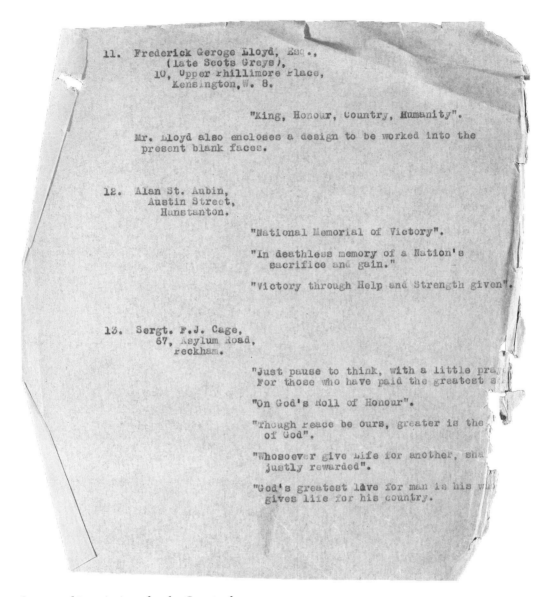

11. Frederick Geroge Lloyd, Esq.,
        (late Scots Greys),
        10, Upper Phillimore Place,
        Kensington, W. 8.

                    "King, Honour, Country, Humanity".

        Mr. Lloyd also encloses a design to be worked into the
        present blank faces.

12. Alan St. Aubin,
        Austin Street,
        Hunstanton.

                    "National Memorial of Victory".

                    "In deathless memory of a Nation's
                        sacrifice and gain."

                    "Victory through Help and Strength given".

13. Sergt. F.J. Cage,
        67, Asylum Road,
        Peckham.

                    "Just pause to think, with a little pray
                    For those who have paid the greatest s

                    "On God's Roll of Honour".

                    "Though peace be ours, greater is the
                        of God".

                    "Whosoever give Life for another, sha
                        justly rewarded".

                    "God's greatest love for man is his wh
                        gives life for his country.

Suggested inscriptions for the Cenotaph. *WORK 20/139*

He stated that the flags which fluttered in the breeze seemed more fitting for those who mourned; and that was enough for him, as he always thought of the Cenotaph as their memorial. That is why he welcomed seeing the fresh piles of flowers placed around it. For him, that symbolised that the Cenotaph had passed from the domain of ceremony, and into the human realm of loving remembrance.

Cenotaph. *WORK 20/139*

Bermuda Cenotaph. *CAOG 10/87*

Unveiling of the Cenotaph in Gambia, 1922. *CO 1069/25*

The Cenotaph was unveiled on Armistice Day in 1920, the same day as the ceremony for the grave of the Unknown Warrior in Westminster. Within a week, more than 1 million people had visited the memorial.[9] The design inspired hundreds of other Cenotaphs around the world. In London, it has become the place where the Remembrance Day ceremony is now held every year.

Memorials to the First World War have appeared around the world in their thousands. From local plaques on walls, to memorials imaged on the Whitehall Cenotaph – something commemorating this conflict is never far away.

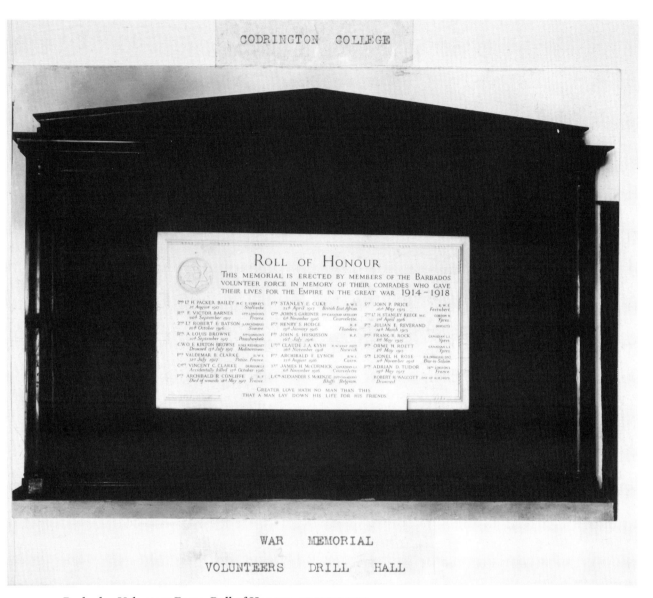

Barbados Volunteer Force, Roll of Honour. *CO 1069/245/25*

THE BATTLE OF FALKLAND ISLANDS

WAR MEMORIAL

Battle of the Falkland Islands war memorial. *CO 1069/313*

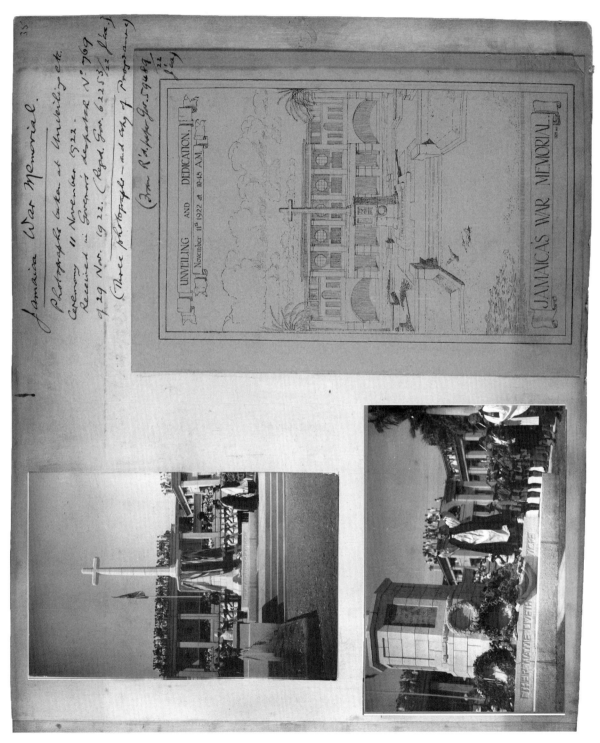

Unveiling of Jamaican war memorial, 1922. *CO 1069/369*

Unveiling of the war memorial in Trinidad and Tobago. *CO 1069/392*

Hong Kong Cenotaph. *CO 1069/476*

Levuka war memorial, Fiji. *CO 1069/647*

Fijian Labour Corps war memorial. *CO 1069/647*

WAR MEMORIAL.

War memorial, Gibraltar. *CO 1069/709*

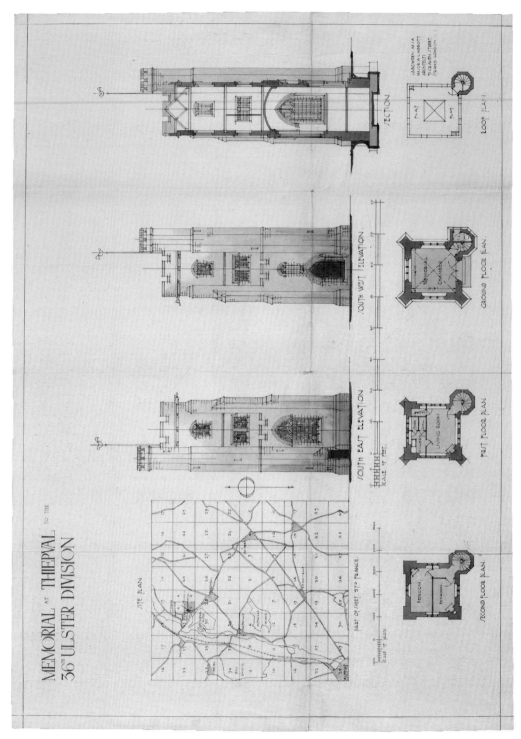

Plans for the war memorial for the 36th Ulster Division, at Thiepval. *WO 32/5868*

Royal Artillery war memorial, Hyde Park Corner. *WORK 20/151*

Royal Artillery war memorial, Hyde Park Corner. *WORK 20/151*

ENDNOTES

Introduction

1. Schattenberg, Susanne: Brest-Litovsk, Treaty of, in: 1914-1918-online. International Encyclopedia of the First World War, ed. by Ute Daniel, Peter Gatrell, Oliver Janz, Heather Jones, Jennifer Keene, Alan Kramer, and Bill Nasson, issued by Freie Universität Berlin, Berlin 2014-11-30.
2. Lloyd, Nick, *Hundred Days: The End of the Great War* (London: Viking, 2013) p.254.
3. David, Saul, *100 Days: How the Great War was Fought and Won* (United Kingdom: Hodder & Stoughton, 2013) p.465.

Treaties

1. Reynolds, David, *The Long Shadow: The Great War and the Twentieth Century* (Great Britain: Simon & Schuster UK Ltd, 2013) p.2.
2. Sharp, Alan: The Paris Peace Conference and its Consequences, in: 1914-1918-online. International Encyclopedia of the First World War, ed. by Ute Daniel, Peter Gatrell, Oliver Janz, Heather Jones, Jennifer Keene, Alan Kramer, and Bill Nasson, issued by Freie Universität Berlin, Berlin 2014-10-08.
3. 'Treaty of Versailles' at https://www.britannica.com/event/Treaty-of-Versailles-1919
4. Haslinger, Peter: Saint-Germain, Treaty of, in: 1914-1918-online. International Encyclopedia of the First World War, ed. by Ute Daniel, Peter Gatrell, Oliver Janz, Heather Jones, Jennifer Keene, Alan Kramer, and Bill Nasson, issued by Freie Universität Berlin, Berlin 2016-12-06.
5. Minkov, Stefan Marinov: Neuilly-sur-Seine, Treaty of, in: 1914-1918-online. International Encyclopedia of the First World War, ed. by Ute Daniel, Peter Gatrell, Oliver Janz, Heather Jones, Jennifer Keene, Alan Kramer, and Bill Nasson, issued by Freie Universität Berlin, Berlin 2017-02-20.
6. Zeidler, Miklós: Trianon, Treaty of, in: 1914-1918-online. International Encyclopedia of the First World War, ed. by Ute Daniel, Peter Gatrell, Oliver Janz, Heather Jones, Jennifer Keene, Alan Kramer, and Bill Nasson, issued by Freie Universität Berlin, Berlin 2014-10-08.
7. Smith, Leonard V.: Post-war Treaties (Ottoman Empire/ Middle East), in: 1914-1918-online. International Encyclopedia of the First World War, ed. by Ute Daniel, Peter Gatrell, Oliver Janz, Heather Jones, Jennifer Keene, Alan Kramer, and Bill Nasson, issued by Freie Universität Berlin, Berlin 2014-10-08.

Demobilisation

1. Reynolds, David, *The Long Shadow: The Great War and the Twentieth Century* (Great Britain: Simon & Schuster UK Ltd, 2013) p.60.
2. TNA: LAB 2/1516/DRA128/30/1918
3. Storey, Neil R. And Housego, Molly, *Women in the First World War* (United Kingdom: Shire Publications Ltd, 2013) p.38.
4. TNA: LAB 2/1516/DRA128/30/1918
5. Ibid.
6. Ibid.
7. LAB 2/1516/DRA129/6/1918
8. Ibid.
9. LAB 2/1516/DRA129/7/1918
10. Ibid.
11. Ibid.
12. LAB 2/1516/DRA129/6/1918
13. Ibid.
14. LAB 2/1516/DRA128/47/1918
15. Ibid.
16. LAB 2/1516/DRA129/6/1918
17. LAB 2/1516/DRA128/19/1918
18. Ibid.

Women's Uniformed Services

1. TNA: AIR 1/105/15/9/284
2. AIR 1/106/15/9/284
3. AIR 8/1741
4. Ibid.
5. ADM 116/3739
6. Ibid.

Disability

1. TNA: LAB 2/1195/TDS2884/1919
2. Cohen, Deborah, *The War Come Home: Disabled Veterans in Britain and Germany, 1914-1939* (California: University of California Press, 2001) p.1.
3. LAB 2/1195/TDS2884/1919
4. Ibid.
5. Ibid.
6. Ibid.

7. Reid, John, *The Princess Louise Scottish Hospital for Limbless Sailors and Soldiers at Erskine House* (Glasgow: James Maclehose and Sons, 1917) p.44.
8. Guyatt, Mary, 'Better Legs: Artificial Limbs for British Veterans of the First World War,' in *Journal of Design History,* vol.14 no.4. Technology and the Body (2001) p.311.
9. Ibid.
10. MUN 7/285
11. LMA, Correspondence About Use Of 'Certalmid' At Roehampton House (1920-1921) H2/QM/A17/10.
12. LMA, News Cuttings No.2., *Evening News*, June 1918.
13. Ibid.
14. Ibid. *Daily Mail*, February 1921.
15. Ibid.
16. Guyatt, p.312.
17. LMA, News Cuttings No. 2., The Times, October 1918.
18. Ibid., Morning Post, December 1918.
19. Ibid.
20. Calder, John, *The Vanishing Willows: The Story of Erskine Hospital* (Bishopton: The Princess Louise Scottish Hospital (Erskine Hospital) 1982) p.16.
21. Guyatt, p.314.
22. Ibid.
23. Ibid., p.315.
24. LMA, News Cuttings No.1. Daily Mail, June 1916.
25. Ibid.
26. Reznick, Jeffrey, *Healing the Nation: Soldiers and the Culture of Caregiving in Britain During the Great War* (Manchester: Manchester University Press, 2004) p.116.
27. John Galsworthy, 'So Comes the Sacred Work', *American Journal Of Care For Cripples,* VII.2 (1918) p.88.
28. Anderson, Julie, *War, Disability and Rehabilitation in Britain: 'Soul of a Nation'* (Manchester: Manchester University Press, 2011) p.31.
29. Ibid. p.57.
30. LMA, News Cuttings No.1. Daily Mail, August 1916.
31. Ibid., Daily Mirror, August 1916.
32. Jones, Edgar, Palmer, Ian and Wessely, Simon, 'War pensions (1900-1945): changing models of psychological understanding' in *British Journal of Psychiatry* 180 (2002) p.374.
33. Bogacz, Ted, 'War Neurosis and Cultural Change in England, 1914-22: The Work of the War Office Committee of Enquiry into 'Shell-Shock" in *Journal of Contemporary History,* vol.24 (1989) p.227.
34. WO 32/4748

Peace Day
1. TNA: WORK 21/74
2. Ibid.
3. Ibid.
4. Ibid.
5. Ibid.
6. Ibid.
7. Ibid.
8. Ibid.

The Unknown Warrior
1. TNA: WORK 20/1/3
2. 'Unknown Warrior' at https://www.westminster-abbey.org/abbey-commemorations/ commemorations/ unknown-warrior/
3. Ibid.
4. Crane, David, *Empires of the Dead: How One Man's Vision Led to the Creation of WW1's War Graves* (London: William Collins, 2014) p.249.
5. Ibid. p.250.
6. WORK 31/2252
7. WO 32/3000
8. Ibid.
9. Ibid.
10. 'Unknown Warrior'

The Cenotaph
1. TNA: WORK 20/139
2. WORK 20/1/3
3. Ibid.
4. Ibid.
5. Ibid.
6. Ibid.
7. WORK 20/139
8. Ibid.
9. Prysor, Glyn: Cenotaph in: 1914-1918-online. International Encyclopedia of the First World War, ed. by Ute Daniel, Peter Gatrell, Oliver Janz, Heather Jones, Jennifer Keene, Alan Kramer, and Bill Nasson, issued by Freie Universität Berlin, Berlin 2014-10-08.

INDEX